Patrick Montana, Ph.D.,
Professor of Management
Hofstra University

Management

New York • London • Toronto • Sydney

All inquiries should be addressed to:
Barron's Educational Series, Inc.
250 Wireless Boulevard
Hauppauge, New York 11788

Library of Congress Catalog Card No. 90-27728

International Standard Book No. 0-8120-4606-4

Library of Congress Cataloging-in-Publication Data
Montana, Patrick J.
    Study keys to management / Patrick Montana.
      p. cm. —(Barron's study keys)
    Includes index.
    ISBN 0-8120-4606-4
    1. Management—Study and teaching. 2. Management.
      I. Title.
  II. Series.
  HD30.4.M66   1991   90-27728
  658'.0076—dc20   CIP

PRINTED IN THE UNITED STATES OF AMERICA

1234   5500   987654321

CONTENTS

Theme 1 DEFINITION AND OVERVIEW OF MANAGEMENT

*A*fter the Industrial Revolution, management evolved as a separate and distinct discipline. Its scope, role, and basic theories have changed over the years, but its purpose—ensuring that the goals of a business or organization are met and productivity and efficiency maximized—remain the same.

This section provides an overview of management—what it is and how it works. Later sections give more detailed outlines of the various aspects of management.

INDIVIDUAL KEYS IN THIS THEME

1 Management and the managerial role

2 The functions of management

3 Management skills

4 Special management systems

Key 1 Management and the managerial role

OVERVIEW *Effective management depends on understanding the role and functions of a manager, the management process, and delegation—the key to getting accountability and results.*

Definition of management: The definition of management has evolved over the years. A currently accepted definition is that of the American Management Association: *Management is working with and through other people to accomplish the objectives of both the organization and its members.*

Emphasis of the definition: Three points in the definition should be emphasized:
- The emphasis is on the people in the organization.
- The attention is focused on objectives and results, not activities.
- Members' personal objectives are integrated with the objectives of the organization

Management activities: Involve getting results through others by the process of **delegation**.

Technical activities: Special functions of an individual following a specific vocational field. As an individual advances in an organization and as management activities and demands increase, involvement in the technical or vocational activities of the organization should decrease. *Example:* A salesperson who becomes a sales manager spends less time selling and more time managing.

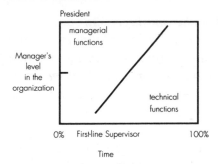

Managerial and technical activities at different levels of management.

First-line supervisors spend about thirty percent of their time in managerial activities and the remainder in technical activities. Presidents should spend at least ninety percent of their time on managerial activities and little or no time on technical activities.

Management process: The management process, no matter what the technical or vocational field, includes the following steps:
1. Set objectives.
2. Assign responsibility and delegate authority.
3. Allocate resources.
4. Design controls and ways to monitor progress.
5. Solve problems as they occur.
6. Evaluate performance and outcome.

Results and accountability: A manager gets results through others by the process of **delegation**. Although a manager cannot delegate ultimate responsibility, he/she can delegate authority. **By sharing responsibility through assignment and delegating authority**, a manager can hold people at other levels in the organization **accountable** for getting things done. Responsibility is the obligation to perform certain duties. Accountability is the obligation to account for results.

Key 2 The functions of management

OVERVIEW *The management process comprises five basic functions, or activities: planning, organizing, staffing, leading, and controlling. Each of these functions relates to every other activity, and in a coordinated way, they progress in a cyclical and ongoing pattern—always with the goal of obtaining results.*

Management process: The managerial process is cyclical in nature. The basic functions, especially planning and controlling, of one cycle are evaluated and used in planning for the next cycle, usually a budget period.

KEY DIAGRAM

Cyclic nature of the management process

Planning: The process of determining organizational goals and how to achieve them.
- **Strategic planning** involves setting long-term goals and establishing general broad guidelines for obtaining these aims.
- **Operational planning**, or day-to-day planning, involves setting specific measurable objectives for a specific time period (usually a budget period) and establishing schedules and timetables for obtaining these objectives within the overall organizational framework.

Organizing: The process of using resources and personnel in an orderly way to achieve the objectives and long-term goals of the organization. Departmentalization, sharing responsibility through assignment, and delegation of authority are parts of the organizing function.

Staffing: Recruiting and placing qualified personnel needed for the organization to achieve its objectives and goals. Selection, compensation, and labor relations are all part of the staffing function.

Leading: Working with people to get them to perform in ways that will help the organization achieve its goals. Communication and motivation are important leadership skills.

Controlling: Making sure that the objectives and goals of an organization are met on a day-to-day basis. Controlling involves setting performance standards for individuals, measuring performance against these standards, and taking action to correct any weaknesses and address any problems. The function of control involves both management control (ensuring the efficient and effective use of human resources) and operational control (ensuring that specific tasks are carried out). The latter is accomplished primarily through scheduling and establishing procedures.

System for managing for results: A management system that attains the desired results has four important links: 1. defining objectives, 2. assigning responsibilities, 3. developing standards of performance, and 4. appraising performance.

KEY DIAGRAM

A system for managing for results.

Hierarchy of Objectives: As each unit in an organization sets its particular objectives, a hierarchy develops with the objectives of one unit affecting those of the units above and below it.

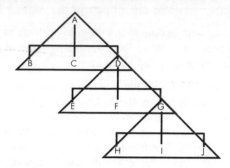

Hierarchy of objectives.

Key 3 Management skills

OVERVIEW *Certain skills are essential if a manager is to succeed in having the organization accomplish its goals. Among these skills are communication, decision making, motivation, knowing how to deal with groups and with conflict situations, and, perhaps most important, time management.*

Communication skills: Communication is essential for organizational success. Without it, a manager cannot bridge the gap between higher management and subordinates and cannot plan, explain, motivate, or lead subordinates.

Motivation: Since the art of management is working with and through people to accomplish goals, a manager must be able to motivate people. Motivation is the process of stimulating an individual or group to work to accomplish the desired goals.

Decision-making: All managers must make decisions. To help them in decision-making, they must be aware of different ways of thinking and approaching decisions and how varying conditions can alter decision-making.

Time management: As managers move up the organizational hierarchy, they should spend more time in managerial tasks, delegating responsibility, and less time in operating or vocational tasks.

Dealing with conflict: An effective manager must be able to resolve conflict—whether the conflict is between individuals or groups or between two or more points of view—in such a way that the outcome leads to the achievement of the organization's objectives.

Dealing with groups: Groups have their own special dynamics—be they large formal groups or committees or small informal groups. An effective manager must appreciate the characteristics of the group and deal with them effectively.

Key 4 Special management systems

OVERVIEW *As the science of management has grown, various approaches and systems have been developed. Among these are Production and Operations Management (POM) systems and Management Information Systems (MIS). International trade and multinational companies have led to the development of International Management as a discipline with special concerns and problems.*

Production and Operations Management (POM): A variety of technologies that stress quantitative methods to facilitate better planning, forecasting, scheduling, and controlling in an organization. *Examples:* PERT, CRP, break-even analysis.

Management Information Systems (MIS): A formal method of giving management accurate and timely information about personnel, data, procedures, and equipment to facilitate decision making and the functioning of all parts of the organization. An MIS is usually made up of several subsystems and uses computer technology.

International management: The management of **multinational companies** and the direction of the international relationships of a company. Managers in this field must be aware of the cultures and business practices of the countries with which they are involved and must know how to coordinate these practices with those of their own organization.

Theme 2 HISTORY AND BASIC THEORIES OF MANAGEMENT

*T*here have been effective supervisors and managers directing major projects throughout history. However, it was the Industrial Revolution and the development of light manufacturing and then heavy manufacturing that led to the development of formulated theories of management. The English writer Charles Babbage was perhaps the first to see the need for a systematic approach to work and management, but his ideas were largely ignored until the early 1900s, when Frederick Taylor wrote the *Principles of Scientific Management*. Since that time, several major schools of management thought have emerged, chief among them the Early, or Classical Schools of Management; the Behavioral Approach; the Situational, or Contingency Approach; the Systems Approach, or Operations Research; and Theory Z.

Key 5 Early classical theories of management

OVERVIEW *The first attempts to develop a scientific approach to management focused on improving worker efficiency. Some focused on the nature of the work and how it could be planned, controlled, and managed to improve efficiency. Others focused on the administration of the organization.*

Frederick W. Taylor: While observing pig-iron and steel shop floors over many years, Taylor studied the nature of specific jobs, breaking a task into **basic work units**. Then, through time and motion studies, he determined the **one right way** to do the job. His ideas, described in *Principles of Scientific Management* (1911), were gradually accepted by managers.

Frank (1868–1924) and Lillian Gilbreth (1878–1972): The Gilbreths furthered the ideas of Scientific Management through detailed motion studies that classified actions and body movements of workers doing a specific job, calling the specific actions **therbligs**. To increase worker efficiency, they analyzed the motions and reduced the number of actions required.

Henry L Gantt (1861–1919): Gantt pointed out the need for managers to use realistic work standards based on study and measurement. His pioneering work schedules, now known as Gantt charts, were widely adopted by industry. Gantt also focused on motivation and advocated **production bonuses** for workers who exceeded expected quotas.

Mary Parker Follet (1868–1933): Focusing on how managers deal with conflict, she advocated a **collaborative approach to problem solving**, rather than overmanagement, or **"bossism."** She believed that workers could understand the "law of the situation," or logic in a management request, and that through **compromise**, conflicts could be resolved.

Henri Fayol (1841–1925): A French engineer, Fayol focused on the organization rather than the worker and defined the overall functions of management (planning, organizing, commanding, coordinating, and controlling). He formulated basic principles of management in *General and Industrial Management* (1929).

Key 6 The behavioral approach
to management

OVERVIEW *The Behavioral Approach to Management focused on the worker, not on the work itself, and had a major impact on the development of management theory.*

Elton Mayo: Through a series of experiments known as the **Hawthorne Studies** (1927–32), Mayo and his colleagues found that worker productivity is related to social and psychological factors as well as the work itself and the physical environment. They found, for example, that when workers knew they were being observed as part of an experiment, their productivity increased—a phenomenon now known as the **Hawthorne Effect**. Calling on managers to consider human relations factors, Mayo focused on people-management skills and is now considered the founder of the **Human Relations Movement**.

Chester Barnard: Focusing on the need for cooperation within an organization, Barnard pointed out that workers accept a managerial directive only if it is acceptable in terms of their personal interests. This **acceptance theory of authority** stressed the need for effective managerial communication and motivation skills and emphasized that managers real power comes not from their position but from the acceptance of the workers.

Douglas M. McGregor: Summarizing the work-focused views of such classical schools as **Theory X** and the worker-focused views of the early behaviorists as **Theory Y**, McGregor crystallized the basic philosophical differences between the two approaches. Advocating the optimistic and **humanistic approaches** of Theory Y, McGregor urged increased concentration on workers, summarized in *The Human Side of Enterprise* (1960).

Key 7 Management science, or
operations research

OVERVIEW *The need to manage increasingly complex organizations and operations led to the use of scientific methodology and mathematical models to research the operations of an organization and determine solutions to specific problems. With this approach an organization is viewed as a complex system composed of interrelated subsystems.*

Early operations research: Spurred by the need to manage the vast World War II military and industrial structure and later the complex post-war industrial technology, operations research groups applied **scientific methods**—observe, construct a **mathematical model**, make deductions under different assumed conditions, and experiment—to determine solutions to complex problems. Operations Research gradually evolved into the Management Science approach to management.

Herbert Simon: Information is essential to effective Management Science. Carnegie-Melon Management scientist Herbert Simon (1978 Nobel laureate in Economics) and his colleagues pointed out that managers need complete and perfect information to make decisions that can achieve maximal results.

Systems approach: Management Science views an organization as a unified but complex **system composed of interrelated subsystems**. Systems theory states that the activity of any subsystem of an organization affects all other subsystems of the organization.

Key 8 The situational, or contingency, approach

OVERVIEW *The **contingency approach** is an eclectic approach to management, borrowing techniques of other approaches if and when those techniques contribute to the attainment of management goals in a particular situation at a particular time.*

Problem-solving methodology: To determine a solution to a specific problem, the contingency approach follows a **step-by-step methodology**:
1. Situational analysis, studying the strengths and weaknesses of the organization itself and analyzing the potential threats to or opportunities for the organization
2. Statement of the problem
3. Statement of measurable objectives and standards for solving the problem
4. Development and evaluation of several possible solutions to the problem
5. Choice of a solution
6. Putting the solution in operation, first on a pilot basis and then, after necessary refinements, into the organizational framework
7. Evaluation of the solution

Factors to be considered: The contingency approach considers:
- factors limiting an organization in environmental, technological, and human relations areas
- impact of a plan or solution not only on the specific problem but on the organization as a whole
- need for flexible managers with a wide-ranging knowledge of many management techniques
- availability of workers, their skills, abilities, and flexibility.

Key 9   Theory Z

OVERVIEW   *Theory Z, based largely on the Japanese approach to management, stresses long-term commitment, worker-management cooperation and discussion, and decision making that takes group consensus into account. The theories of Mayo and McGregor (See Key 6), focusing on the nature of the worker and the human dimension of work, and the work of Herzberg on motivation contributed to the development of theory Z.*

Group consensus: Theory Z believes in group decision making, based on the assumptions that a group has access to more information and experience than an individual and that group dynamics will filter out the extreme opinions and result in a decision that all members of the group can accept and support.

Lifetime employment: In an effort to guarantee a committed and experienced long-term work force, Japanese managers view their workers as lifetime employees. Employees are periodically evaluated on their performance and accomplishments.

Quality of worklife (QWL) approach: Characterized by frequent worker-management communication, worker control over some parts of the workplace, and worker participation in facets of decision making.

Quality Circle (QC): A small group of workers and managers that meets on a regular basis to discuss ways to improve quality and decrease costs and to formulate suggestions that are then forwarded to higher management levels. This is a specific technique in the QWL approach.

Factors affecting the QWL approach: Factors influencing the overall effectiveness and success of a QWL approach include:
- the cost of worker time
- the need for workers and management alike to be able to communicate effectively
- the attitude and support of top-level management.

Theme 3   MANAGEMENT AND ITS ENVIRONMENT

*N*o organization is self-contained, existing in a vacuum. All organizations relate to and are affected by their environment—both their internal environment and their external environment. How an organization relates to social and public concerns in its external environment—its social responsiveness—has long been and continues to be a subject of interest and controversy.

Key 10 External environment
of business

OVERVIEW *The external environment of a business consists of those factors outside the organization that affect the organization and are relevant to its operation.*

Political factors: Political factors influence a business through the **local, state, and federal laws** that affect the operation of the business. *Examples:* consumer protection laws, stock market and banking regulations, interstate commerce laws, environmental protection laws, antidiscrimination laws, and government spending.

Sociological factors: The values and culture of a nation affect the way people feel about the organization they are in and about work itself. Added to this are individual values and work ethic. Changes in the nature of a population—for example, an aging population, a less educated population, or the movement of people to different parts of the country—are also important sociological factors.

Direct economic factors: Economic factors having a **direct** and **immediate effect** on a business are number and actions of competitors, availability and costs of supplies, number and behavior of customers (target market), actions of shareholders in the company, and relationships with financial institutions.

Indirect economic factors: Factors having an **indirect** or less immediate **effect** on business are aspects of the nation's economy, such as rate of inflation or recession, interest rates, unemployment rate, gross national product (GNP), and standard of living.

Technological factors: Technological change can have a profound and immediate effect on business, often necessitating such changes as the expenditure of capital on new equipment and the reeducation of employees. A useful technique is to introduce the innovation in a gradual, or step-by-step, way.

External environment: No organization is self-contained or self-sufficient. An organization takes in **inputs** (raw materials, money, labor), **transforms** them into products or services, and provides **outputs** (finished products, services, etc.) to the environment. This concept is sometimes called an **open systems model**.

Key 11 Internal environment of business

OVERVIEW *The resources within an organization, used to achieve its goal, make up the **internal environment** of a business. Financial, technological, human, and physical resources are needed.*

Financial resources: An organization must obtain funds to provide for its operation and growth. Funds are commonly obtained through borrowing (**debt capital** from loans or bonds), through the selling of stock in the company (**equity capital**), or through retaining funds already earned (**retained earnings**).

Human resources: The organization must hire the required workers, and then assign, train, and motivate them to attain the objectives set by management.

Physical resources: The physical resources of an organization include the plant, manufacturing and production equipment, office space, distribution and sales facilities, and inventory of raw materials. Accessibility of raw materials, work force, and markets must be considered in the location of the resources.

Technological resources: The level of technology and skill of the employees in a firm are used to transform inputs to outputs. Management must decide the appropriate level of technology and innovation for its particular business.

Key 12 Does management have a social responsibility?

OVERVIEW *The appropriate level of social responsibility by business has been a subject of controversy for decades. In fact, some question whether business has any social obligation at all and whether it should involve itself in any social actions.*

Background: The view that business should pursue profits with little or no regard for social needs has gradually changed over the past fifty years. Fueled by the consumer and environmental movements, a host of laws safeguard the public and regulate many business activities. However, the basic question, "Does Management have a social responsibility?" remains.

Arguments against social responsibility: Associated with Nobel laureate (Economics 1976) Milton Friedman and others:
- Managers are obligated to maximize profits for their shareholders and cannot legally divert funds for other purposes.
- Business leaders are not qualified to make social decisions or expert at how to achieve social goals.
- The money spent by a business on social problems would decrease profits, result in higher consumer prices, and decrease capital available for innovation and improvement, thereby decreasing competitive advantages.
- Social problems are the concern of government, not business, and a linking of government and business in social endeavors would be unhealthy.

Arguments for social responsibility: Associated with economist Keith Davis and others:
- Business has the ethical obligation to involve itself in social and public concerns in areas where it shares some responsibility: environmental pollution, job discrimination, product hazards.
- If business does not act responsibly on social issues, it will face greater government intervention.
- Social responsibility and action on social issues improves a company's public image, and this, in turn, may benefit the company.
- Business should act on small problems now to prevent their becoming major problems that will invariably have deleterious effects on all aspects of society, including business.

Key 13   Degrees of social responsibility

OVERVIEW   *The extent to which an organization responds to social concerns is its **social responsiveness**. Various approaches and levels of commitment have evolved, forming a continuum or response from least, or minimally involved, to most involved.*

Obligation: Obey the law: Those believing in a minimal business role in social action hold that the only obligation of a business is to obey the law and do only what it requires. In this approach, sometimes called the Social Obligation Theory, minimal resources are given to social concerns and no voluntary efforts are made.

Responsibility: Obey the law and react to the public: At this level of social responsibility, managers go beyond the minimum of obeying the pertinent laws. They actively seek public opinion and **react to public concerns**. While safeguarding company profits, they react to problems affecting their community and contribute to social efforts, maintaining a good public image for the company.

Responsiveness: Obey, react, and anticipate: At this highest level of social responsiveness, managers actively **anticipate public expectations** and establish high standards of social conduct and action for their business, thereby creating higher public expectations of future social responsibility and action on the part of businesses. This social responsiveness approach uses the resources and power of a business to attempt to improve society as a whole.

Key 14 Areas of social concern

OVERVIEW *Social action by business has largely been concentrated in several areas: air pollution, water pollution, solid waste disposal, and noise pollution, with many of the business actions mandated or regulated by local, state, and federal laws. Conditions of employment have also been a major focus of social action.*

Air pollution: Since the 1950s, the U.S. government has enacted a series of laws mandating the participation of business in the improvement of air quality. Businesses in many fields have established different types of air-cleaning technologies to fulfill their obligations.

Water pollution: Legislation has also imposed obligations on business in the area of water quality. *Example:* Manufacturing firms must control industrial effluents and prevent further degradation of water quality.

Solid waste management: Solid waste—garbage, hazardous waste, radioactive wastes, etc.—is also a problem area. Stringent government regulations monitor the disposal of all radioactive and hazardous wastes and regulate other aspects of solid waste disposal.

Noise pollution: The Noise Control Act of 1972 requires business to control noise levels by moving the source of the noise, redesigning equipment, or otherwise muffling the noise.

Conditions of employment: Prodded by civil rights legislation, businesses are following practices of **equal opportunity** and **affirmative action** in all employment practices. Worker safety and protection are addressed under regulations of the federal Occupational Safety and Health Act (OSHA).

Key 15 Managing social action

OVERVIEW *No matter what the level of an organization's social responsiveness, it must proceed through an orderly and organized **action stage** and **evaluation stage** in all its social actions.*

Identification of a social need: In the first step, a social situation is studied to identify problems, determine goals, and **establish standards**.

Choice of a course of action: After a need has been identified and standards set, alternative plans are analyzed in terms of their potential effectiveness, costs to the organization, and likely consequences. Then, a plan of action is chosen.

Execution of the plan: Once a course of action is decided on, if feasible, a pilot test may be run. Revisions are then made and the plan put into full operation.

Evaluation: A company appraises its social activity through a **social audit**. This may involve a simple listing of the social actions undertaken or a summary of social actions with their costs and their successes in fulfilling the organization's philosophy toward social action. Or, a complex list of social actions, their costs, their successes, and their subsequent benefits to the organization may be done in a **cost-benefit analysis**.

Theme 4 PLANNING

*P*lanning is the process of determining organizational goals and how to achieve them. It is one of the five major functions of management. The importance of planning cannot be overestimated. It is a continuum essential to the success and growth of any organization. Planning itself must be planned and carried out through an organized and orderly process. Various approaches, techniques, and tools have been developed to help in the planning process. All focus on the cooperation and understanding of responsibilities between management and employees in attaining the goals of the organization.

Key 16 Planning—importance and process

OVERVIEW *The setting of overall **managerial strategy** is the first step in recognizing the importance of planning and setting the different levels of planning into operation in an organization. Continual review of the strategy in terms of the market response leads to future successful planning.*

Importance: Without planning, an organization may be overwhelmed by competition or find its position overtaken by new ideas, markets, or products. Today's organizations are too complex for "seat-of-the-pants" decision making. Planning forces managers to think through issues and alternatives.

Description: Planning can be described as 1. choosing a destination; 2. evaluating alternative routes to that destination; and 3. deciding on a specific course to follow.

Process and continuum: Planning is carried out at all levels of management in an orderly process and on a continuing basis.

Tailored to each organization: Although the basic concepts of planning are the same, each organization's philosophy and culture results in a different set of priorities. Communication and staff involvement at different levels of planning are essential for success.

Management strategy: The setting of long-term goals and objectives of the organization, allocating resources, and adopting those basic courses of action necessary to attain the goals.

Steps in setting management strategy: Setting the long-term strategy of an organization can be broken down into five steps:
1. Identify a market opportunity, or what an organization might do.
2. Evaluate what the organization can do with its resources and capabilities.
3. Decide what to do in terms of the values and interests of the organization's executives.
4. Determine what the organization should do in terms of its obligations to society.
5. Match opportunities, obligations, resources, and capabilities with an acceptable level of risk to set a specific goal in a **Mission Statement**, or **Statement of Purpose**.

Criteria for evaluating managerial strategy: Once a strategy has been adopted, management must review it in terms of market response and make appropriate changes. Key questions for evaluating basic strategy include:

- Does the strategy fully explore the marketing opportunities?
- Are the major operational policies derived from the strategy still consistent with the overall goals?
- Does the strategy stimulate organizational effort?

Key 17   Levels and tools of planning

OVERVIEW   *Planning is carried out at different levels within an organization and with different specific functions. Charts, tables, and computer-assisted analyses are among the techniques and tools that can be used to aid in planning.*

KEY DIAGRAM

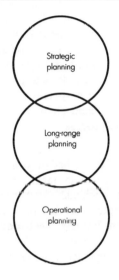

Hierarchy of planning.

Planning framework: In general, there are three levels of planning, each with some overlap, but each involving a different time frame and a different level of detail.

- **Strategic planning** addresses the organization's **basic mission** or business, issuing very **broad statements** of purpose or direction that have a **long lead time.** *Example:* Mission Statements.
- **Long-range planning** is **middle-level planning** that, within a **shorter time frame,** looks specifically at resources, finances, and market conditions to determine **ways to accomplish the overall strategic plans of the organization.**
- Operational, or **day-to-day, planning** involves managers in each unit of an organization who are responsible for achieving the unit's

objectives within a specified period of time—say, one year or one budget period—through the use of **measurable targets**, **schedules**, **timetables**, etc.

Planning function: Planning can also be viewed as a function of the organization. Planning is done on the corporate level and on lower individual levels with each manager planning for his or her unit.

- **Corporate level planning:** Often done by a separate planning department or task force, this coordinates, facilitates, and provides staff support for line executives. Data from the organization's external environment that may affect the overall mission and strategic planning of the organization are gathered, analyzed, and prepared for use by the line executives and unit managers who do the actual planning. *Examples:* legislation affecting the organization's business, economic trends, the rise of a new competitor.
- **Managerial level planning:** Each manager uses the data supplied by the corporate planning task force and the directives of higher management to plan exactly how to **phase a project from idea to implementation within a specified time frame**. Each manager uses tools, including Gantt charts and scheduling techniques, to help in the planning process.

Planning tools:
- **Gantt Charts** are used to schedule work. (See Key 5.) A project is broken down into separate tasks, and estimates of the time required to complete each task and its required completion date are combined in a graphic chart that facilitates work scheduling.
- **Project Evaluation Review Technique** (PERT) is a network analysis that enables managers to determine the correct and economically efficient sequence of tasks in the completion of a complex project.
- **Critical Path Method (CPM)** is a network analysis tool that enables managers to analyze potential bottlenecks in a project.

Key 18 Provisional planning—GAP analysis

OVERVIEW *GAP analysis is a planning approach for determining where an organization is today, where it wants to go, and how it is going to get there.*

Identifying a GAP: Determine where the organization is today in terms of strategic planning, where it is heading at its present momentum, and where it wants to go. The GAP between its present momentum and its potential is a **planning gap**.

KEY DIAGRAM

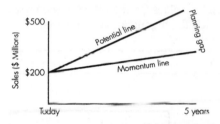

GAP analysis. A planning gap exists between the momentum of organization—where it is going—and its potential—where it wants to go.

Filling the GAP: There are four ways to fill a planning gap:
1. improve current operations;
2. develop new products or services;
3. develop new markets;
4. diversify.

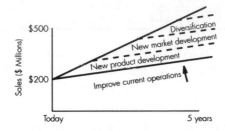

Filling the planning gap. The GAP between momentum and potential can be filled by improving current operations, by developing new products and markets, and by diversifying.

Product market matrix: A tool used to analyze ways of filling a planning gap. The goal is to balance markets, products, the momentum of the present, and the plans for the future in such a way as to maximize growth and reach the organization's potential.

KEY DIAGRAM

		Markets	
--	--	Present	New
Products	Present	Momentum	New Market Development
	New	New Product Development	Diversification

Filling the planning gap by analyzing the product market matrix.

Key 19   Assessing preparedness—
SWOT approach

OVERVIEW *The SWOT approach is an approach to pro-*
visional planning that assesses an organization's strengths
(S), weaknesses (W), opportunities (O) and threats (T), usu-
ally through interviewing executives and gathering informa-
tion.

Step One—interview and gather information: The interviewer ex-
plains the purpose of the interview, assures all interviewees of con-
fidentiality, and then asks:
- What is a strength or is satisfactory in the organization? (Interviewees explain their opinions and provide references to support
  their idea.)
- What is a weakness in the operation? (Again, ask for support.)
- What is a future opportunity?
- What is a possible threat to the organization?

Step Two—organize data: The manager organizes the data gathered,
using a SWOT matrix to determine what must be done to safeguard
the strengths of the organization, what must be done to overcome the
weaknesses, and what must be done to take advantage of the opportunities and avoid the threats.

KEY DIAGRAM

What is	Present Operations	Future Operations
Good	Strengths	Opportunities
Bad	Weaknesses	Threats

SWOT matrix.

Step Three—provide feedback: After analyzing the data and determining future plans, the manager provides feedback to those executives
interviewed. This step helps to ensure their cooperation in implementing the future plans.

Key 20   Management by objectives:
Setting and evaluating objectives

OVERVIEW   *One planning approach is Management by Objectives, a system that sets achievable objectives and has specific criteria for evaluating these objectives. To attain the objectives, management assigns responsibilities and sets standards by which performance and the attainment of objectives are appraised.*

Management by Objectives: a systematic and organized approach that allows management to focus on achievable goals and to attain the best results from available resources.

Types of objectives: There are three main types:
- **Routine Objectives** are ongoing, continuing from year to year.
- **Innovative Objectives** involve solving a particular problem, starting a new project, or similar nonrecurrent situation.
- **Improvement Objectives** require improving performance over that of past years.

Criteria for objectives: To be effective, all objectives must be:
- focused on a *result,* not an activity
- consistent
- specific
- measurable
- related to time
- attainable

Emphasis on "The Result": The emphasis of Management by Objectives is on the result, not on the activity. However, one person's result can be another's activity. At one level in an organization an objective can be a valid result expected, whereas at a higher level that same objective is an activity, not a result.

Key 21 Negotiating and writing
a performance contract

OVERVIEW *By putting into writing the expectations of the manager and the subordinates, a performance contract helps to avoid conflict over different assumptions based on different perspectives.*

Performance contract: Agreement between a manager and subordinates on the responsibilities and standards for the subordinate for a specified period of time (usually a budget period). A performance contract includes a statement of responsibilities and standards of performance.

Statement of responsibilities: Lists those responsibilities for which a particular employee will be held accountable. In general, the higher the level in the organization, the broader the responsibilities; the lower the level, the more specific and detailed the responsibilities.

Standards of performance: Standards of performance are statements of the **results expected** when a specific job or responsibility is completed.

Negotiating a performance contract: A performance contract requires the mutual agreement of manager and subordinate on expectations and objectives. Necessary negotiating steps include:
- agreement and commitment from subordinate on the objectives of the unit
- subordinate's understanding and writing key responsibilities and standards of performance for these responsibilities
- agreement between subordinate and manager on final form of statement of responsibilities and standards of performance

Negotiating tools: To increase the effectiveness of negotiating and help solve problems along the way, different types of questions are useful:
- **Open questions** invite a full expression of thoughts and opinions.
- **Reflection questions**, in which one negotiator rephrases what another negotiator has said, can ensure understanding, create a "climate of agreement," and encourage clarification and additional expression.
- **Directed Question** can clarify positions, provide more information, and focus on areas of agreement.

Key 22 Standards of performance

OVERVIEW *Standards of performance are statements of results expected when a job is completed. They may be objective or subjective.*

Objective standards: Standards based on measurable results. There are three types:
- **Engineered Standards** are essentially a statement of the results each subordinate must achieve so that the manager can achieve the overall objective; usually expressed in a positive way.
- **Historical standards** are standards based on past results. Comparing current results with past results helps in planning future results; usually expressed as a negative.
- **Comparative standards** are based on the results others in the same business are producing; usually expressed as a zero standard.

Expressing objective standards: Each type of objective standard can be expressed in three different ways. However, each type of standard is most commonly expressed in a specific way.
- **Positive standards** state the results desired. *Example:* a quota to be produced each week.
- **Negative standards** state the results not desired but do not express specifically the exact results desired. *Example:* stating a maximum number of errors or rejections that will be tolerated.
- **Zero Standards** state exactly what is not wanted at all. *Example:* "There will be *no* rejections because of . . . ."

Subjective standards: Standards based on the personal preference of the manager and not on any specific measurable result. Subjective standards may include personal preference, prejudice, bias, and intangible criticisms.

Criteria for performance standards: To be effective and useful, performance standards must:
- apply to a single job responsibility
- be specific
- contain a target date for achievement
- be attainable
- be expressed as a result

Theme 5 ORGANIZING

*O*rganizing is the process of using the resources and personnel of an organization in an orderly way to achieve the objectives and long-term goals of the organization. It is one of the five major functions of management. Organization is dependent on delegation of responsibility and authority, the establishment of workable units through departmentalization, and the coordination of these factors into an organizational structure suited to the particular organization.

Key 23   Guidelines for organizing

OVERVIEW   *Organizing is done to help reach goals and objectives. It is a function of planning. Once an organization's goals—managerial strategy—have been established, a structure to carry out the plan is needed, including both formal and informal relationships.*

Unity of purpose: Agreement on what must be done—what functions must be performed. It is the first step in organizing.

Division of labor and staffing: Once there is agreement on what must be done, there must be agreement on who is going to do each task. The type, number, and experience of staff needed must be determined, and the staff organized.

Formation of an organizational framework: The staff must be organized to facilitate teamwork in terms of flow of information and materials and, most importantly, **chain of command**.

Span of control: The number of individual subordinates a manager can effectively supervise. Managers must have time to complete their own tasks as well as counsel, motivate, and control subordinates.

Unity of command: Subordinates should report to only **one boss**, even in large organizations.

Position (job) descriptions: There should be a job description for each particular job to assure an exact understanding of and agreement on responsibilities between manager and subordinate.

Keeping an organization lean and simple: Managers should try to avoid too many levels of review and appraisal. They should structure the organization from a ''need'' basis, not from a ''personnel available'' viewpoint.

Key 24 Departmentalization

OVERVIEW *Departmentalization is the grouping of related activities or functions into manageable units so that the individual units can not only work efficiently to achieve the unit's objectives but also work together to attain the organization's overall goals.*

Methods: Departmentalization can be done in several ways, depending on such factors as the size and nature of the organization, its geographic range, and marketing sphere.

Function: The most common type of departmentalization, especially in smaller companies, is by function, with departments such as finance, marketing, or production. A functional structure makes efficient use of specialized resources and makes supervision easier, but it may lead to slow response time and to a loss of coordination between departments and a loss of final accountability.

Process: In a manufacturing business, departmentalization may occur by process, with departments such as pattern making, fabric cutting, and fabric coloring.

Product: Product departmentalization is used when one product type requires manufacturing and marketing technology different from that used in other parts of the organization. This usually occurs in a large diversified company. *Examples:* large automobile manufacturers, food, or household product manufacturers.

Geography: For a large organization spread throughout the world, departmentalization by geography, bringing together in one department all the activities performed in the region where the unit does its business, may be preferable. Nearness to raw materials, to specialized markets or to a specialized work force may be deciding factors.

Customer/Market: A large diversified company that sells some or all of its products to a particular customer, class of customer, or type of market may departmentalize along those lines. Classes of customers or markets might include the military, educational institutions, or health care facilities.

Matrix/Project: In departmentalization by project, people with different backgrounds, educations, and technical expertise are grouped together to accomplish a specific project within a specified period of time. Pioneered in the aerospace industry, matrix departmentalization has been used for some space projects.

Combination approach: Many organizations, especially large and diversified companies, use a combination of different types of departmentalization to achieve the organizational structure best for them.

Key 23 Delegation and the chain of command

OVERVIEW *Delegation is the art of management, the process of getting results accomplished through others. Delegation involves the principles of responsibility, authority, and accountability, as well as understanding the concept of a chain of command.*

Delegation process: The manager first assigns duties to be performed (**responsibilities**) and gives **authority** commensurate with the responsibilities. Next, the manager develops with the employee standards for the employee's performance (the **accountability** of the employee). The successful accomplishment of the standards should equal the assigned responsibilities.

Risks of delegation: Loss of control, possible loss of a job and **reverse delegation**, when the manager, presented with a problem by a subordinate, takes on the problem and assumes responsibility for the task delegated to the subordinate in the first place.

Techniques: Several techniques facilitate successful delegation, including a clear (preferably written) statement of responsibilities; a periodic rating of performance; and the manager's knowledge of subordinates' qualifications, abilities, motivation, and limitations.

Parity of authority and responsibility: Authority should equal responsibility. If it does not, employee dissatisfaction, wasted time and energy, and frustration will ensue.

Scalar principle: A clearly defined system of authority must exist in an organization. The authority must flow, one link at a time, through a **chain of command** from the top to the bottom of an organization.

Decentralization vs centralization: When a significant amount of authority is delegated to lower levels in an organization, the business id **decentralized**, permitting **faster decision making** with the decision adapted to the particular conditions. When only a limited amount of authority is delegated, the business is **centralized**, characterized by **uniformity** of policies and procedures and close **control**.

Key 26 Types of organizational structures

OVERVIEW *The framework for organizing the relationship of responsibility, authority, and accountability is known as the organizational structure. There are several widely used organizational structure plans as well as other contingent plans, dependent on environmental and technological conditions relating to the organization.*

Structures: There are three major, widely used, organizational frameworks.
- **Line organization**, the simplest organizational structure, has direct **vertical links** between groups in a **scalar chain**, resulting in clear lines of authority and ease of decision making. All units in this type of organization are doers, actively involved in producing or marketing the organization's product or service.

Key Diagram

- **Line and staff organization** uses specialists to advise, service, or support the line in some way. Staff specialists contribute to the efficiency of an organization, but their authority is usually limited to making recommendations to the line organization, and this can occasionally create conflict. Human resources, research and development, and auditing are typical staff functions.

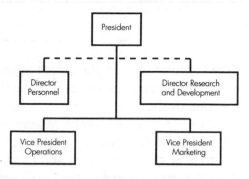

Committee organization: has a group of people appointed to consider certain specific matters. Committees may be **permanent**, or **standing**, often serving in an advisory capacity, or they may be **temporary**, or **ad hoc**, established to consider a specific situation. Certain committees, known as **plural committees**, have the authority to order (not just advise, as most committees do). *Example:* A board of director's executive committee for compensation.

Contingency approach: Several studies showing a relationship between organizational structure and environment and between organizational structure and technology have led to the development of a contingency approach to organization. This approach is **dynamic**, stressing the situation, pace of change, size of an organization, managerial style, and environmental and technological conditions.

Theme 6 STAFFING

*S*taffing is the recruitment and placement of qualified personnel needed in an organization to achieve its goals and objectives. It is one of the five major functions of management. As the field of Human Resource Management developed, basic management theories and governmental regulations combined to give rise to policies and techniques dealing with worker selection, compensation, and separations as well as labor relations in the workplace.

Key 27　Development of human resource management

OVERVIEW　*The management of people—human resources—evolved into a separate field of management as organizations became more complex, labor unions arose, and a host of government regulations entered the work place, influencing manager-subordinate relations.*

Need for managers in a "new" industrial economy: The end of the 19th century saw the shift from agrarian to industrial economy. The beginnings of an assembly line, with one person responsible for only part of a product, created the need for managers to coordinate and oversee the operation of the plant.

Need for specialized managers for personnel: As factories became larger and the workplace more complex, the need arose for managers who specialized in hiring, plant safety, and dealing with workers about working conditions and benefits. The development of on-the-job training programs and the influence of the behavioral approach to management, with its emphasis on workers, furthered the need for human resource specialists.

Rise of unions: During the 1930s, labor unions—organizations to represent workers in their dealings with management—emerged and became increasingly powerful through the 1940s and early 1950s.

Laws affecting labor relations: Starting with the Wagner Act (National Labor Relations Act, 1935), a series of federal laws have recognized unions as legal representatives of workers and have established minimum wage laws and other regulations concerning working conditions.

Key 28   Personnel planning, recruitment, selection, and training

OVERVIEW   *To fulfill their staffing function, managers must plan the personnel needs of the organization, recruit a pool of potential employees, select those best qualified on the basis of job-related factors, and train new employees so that they become effective members of the organization and at the same time progress on their career paths.*

Career path: A series of jobs linked together, each providing skills and/or experience needed for advancement to the next job level in the organization. A path may be **vertical**, consisting of related, sequential jobs leading to higher positions, or **horizontal**, consisting of nonsequential jobs that must be completed before advancement. A manager who remains at one level in a career path, failing to rise further in the organization, is said to have **plateaued**.

Purpose of recruitment: To provide a large enough group of people for a particular position so that the organization can select the best qualified. Recruitment may be general, as when a large pool of typists is needed, or specialized, when a high-level executive with special skills is needed.

Ways to recruit personnel: Personnel may be recruited through ads in newspapers and specialty journals, through public and private employment agencies, through colleges and graduate schools, through executive search ("head-hunter") firms, and through referrals from people within and outside the organization. Within a company, a posting of a **job notice** in a heavily used area and a search of personnel files may reveal employees qualified for the new position.

Selection: The process by which an organization screens and interviews a job candidate and decides whether a specific job offer should be made and what the conditions of the offer should be. The steps in the selection process depend on the particular position and level of the job and may include any or all of the following: initial application or résumé, screening interview, test (e.g., typing), reference and background check, physical examination, and in-depth interview.

Interview: An interview is the key part in the selection process for most management-level positions. A manager conducting an interview must allow sufficient time for the interview, prepare by reviewing the applicant's résumé, and be sure to ask only **job-related questions**. Questions about race, sex, marital status, nationality, religion, political affiliation, or age are illegal.

Types of interviews: Although most interviews include both predetermined questions and open-ended general questions, there are three basic types of interviews:

- **Structured Interview:** Predetermined questions focus on an applicant's knowledge of the job and on ways to handle different aspects of the job under different situations. A standard interview protocol allows comparison of interviewee answers and ensures consistency.

- **Unstructured Interview:** General, open-ended job-related questions are asked.

- **Stress Interview:** The candidate is placed under stress and sometimes asked argumentative questions to determine reactions. This type of interview may not elicit truly worthwhile information and may engender resentment in the candidate.

Training: Training for new employees may include formal or informal orientation meetings, apprenticeship, coaching, on-the-job rotation, or specific schooling, sometimes **on-the-job or** sometimes **off-the-job** through seminars and tuition reimbursement plans.

Key 29 Compensation

OVERVIEW *Compensation is remuneration or reward given to an employee for the performance of a specific job in the form of cash or noncash benefits.*

Cash compensation: Usually in one of the following forms:
- **Salary** is a predetermined amount of money paid for the performance of a specific job over a specified period of time—for example, a week
- **Piece work pay** is money paid per piece, or unit, of work performed. *Example:* $5 per dress sewn.
- **Hourly rate** is money paid according to a specified rate per hour of work time. Hourly rates are used to calculate wages for hours worked in excess of the base number of hours (e.g., 35 or 40 hours a week) for which a salary is paid, and by freelance workers who bill for their services based on the number of hours worked.
- **A bonus** is an extra, infrequent payment to an employee based on the performance of the employee or of the organization during a specified period of time. *Example:* Christmas bonus.

Noncash compensation: Sometimes called **fringe benefits**, include medical and life insurance benefits, tuition-assistance plans, vacation time, retirement pension contributions, and day-care for workers' children. Noncash compensation typically equals approximately 30 percent of salary, with a large percentage of that going to medical insurance.

Influences on compensation: Factors inside and outside the organization influence the rate of compensation. Among the most significant factors are:
- **Unions:** Drawing strength from membership size, tight organization, and affiliation with national unions, local unions typically negotiate with management for salary and noncash benefits for their members.
- **Competition:** The number of qualified and available personnel for a particular job affects the compensation rate, establishing a **going rate** for a particular job in a particular industry and location.
- **Company's profitability:** Obviously a company that is successful is able to pay higher rates than a company in financial distress.
- **Laws:** A variety of federal and state laws have established minimum hourly rates, forbid discrimination or unequal treatment, and set compensation standards and guidelines in certain situations.

Key 30 Labor relations

OVERVIEW *About 20 percent of the U.S. workforce is represented by unions, a drop from almost twice that in the 1940s. Certain basic ideas and procedures are now applied to nonunion worker-management negotiations as well as to union-management dealings, including collective bargaining, mediation, and arbitration.*

Labor union: An organization of workers formed to foster the interests of the members. Through an employee election, the union becomes the legal representative of the workers. As such, the union negotiates with management to secure conditions acceptable to the workers.

Collective bargaining: The process by which management and union representatives negotiate a written contract outlining working conditions (salary, overtime rates, vacation policy, health benefits, etc.), accepting the union as the workers' legal representative, and agreeing upon a procedure for resolving disputes or grievances.

Grievance procedures: A **grievance** is a disagreement or dispute arising from a decision by management or a change in working conditions. The procedures designed to handle grievances differ in different organizations, but most, if not all, require written evidence of the grievance (e.g., a diary or incident log); a meeting with the individual's immediate supervisor; and a series of meetings with higher levels of management. An unresolved grievance may go either to a high-level manager whose decision will be final or to arbitration or mediation.

Mediation: The process in which a neutral outsider—a **mediator**—talks with both sides in an effort to resolve a dispute. The mediator makes a **nonbinding recommendation** to both parties.

Arbitration: The process in which a neutral outsider—an **arbitrator**—reviews the facts of the case, holds a hearing if necessary, and prepares a written decision on the case. Both parties must agree in advance to accept the decision of the arbitrator as final.

Key 31 Separations

OVERVIEW *Separation is the term used to describe the manner in which a person leaves, or separates from, an organization. Separations may be voluntary, involuntary, or mandatory.*

Retirement: Separation from an organization because of advancing age (or illness) can be voluntary or mandatory.
- In **voluntary retirement**, a person decides to leave the organization at a certain age, usually in accordance with the provisions of the organization's retirement benefits plan.
- In **mandatory retirement**, the organization sets a certain age at which employees must retire. Federal law now prohibits mandatory retirement based on any age for employees protected by the law. One exemption, until December 31, 1993, is tenured college professors, who may be required to retire at age 70 unless state law, which may be more strict than federal, forbids compulsory retirement.

Resignation: The employee's voluntary decision to leave an organization. An employee should give management at least two weeks' **notice** of intention to leave.

Reduction in force (cutbacks): Businesses in financial distress may need to reduce their number of employees. By offering early retirement plans, special severance or benefits packages, or other incentives, companies may encourage workers to leave in a **voluntary** manner. In other circumstances, the reductions may be **involuntary** with the **layoff** of certain numbers of people.

Termination (discharge): The most unpleasant form of separation. It is always involuntary, implying a history of poor job performance or violation of company policies and rules.

Theme 7 LEADERSHIP

*L*eadership is the process by which managers motivate, influence, direct, and communicate with subordinates to get them to perform in ways that will help the organization achieve its goals. It is one of the five major functions of management. The ability to influence others—power—in an organization has several sources and levels and can be exercised in a variety of ways. This has led to the development of various schools and techniques of leadership.

Key 32   Power in an organization

OVERVIEW   *To exercise the leadership function of management, a manager must have power or the ability to influence others, specifically subordinates, in the organizational framework. Power is derived from several sources, and a manager's understanding of these sources makes the manager's use of power—and authority—more effective.*

Sources of power: In any organization, power derives from several sources:
- **Legitimate power** is derived from hierarchical structure of the organization and occurs as subordinates recognize the rightful authority of the manager to influence and lead them. Legitimate power is a function of a particular position and stays with the position, not the individual.
- **Reward power** is based on a manager's ability to reward a subordinate for a particular performance—for example, by granting a raise or recommending a promotion.
- **Coercive power** is based on a manager's ability to punish a subordinate. Example: by denying a promotion or raise.
- **Expert power** is based on an individual's knowledge, special skills, abilities, or previous experience valuable to the organization.
- **Referent power** is based on an individual's ability to influence others through personal characteristics or charismatic personality. **Association** can also result in referent power. *Example:* A deputy vice president's power from association with the vice president.
- **Information power** comes from the possession of information important to the organization and its functioning, and may be held by anyone in the organization (e.g., a secretary) who has access to vital information.

Formal vs. informal leaders: In any organization there are **formal leaders**, who lead by virtue of their position, and **informal leaders**, who have no official leadership position but lead by virtue of their personal characteristics, knowledge, or experience.

Power and authority: Although the terms are sometimes used interchangeably, "authority" usually refers to the official power of a manager over subordinates. It can also refer to actions of a subordinate over a manager in a specific situation. *Example:* A guard requiring a manager to show an identity card.

Key 33   Techniques of leadership

OVERVIEW   *Different theories on the nature of leadership and the use of power in an organization have led to the development of several theories and techniques of leadership.*

Trait theory: Holds that the possession of certain personal traits is a hallmark of a leader. In other words, **leaders are born, not made**. Many research studies have failed to identify specific traits that distinguish leaders from nonleaders and further have indicated that leadership traits can be learned.

Behavioral approach: Focusing on what the leader does, not on the traits he or she possesses, the behavioral approach holds that leadership has at least two aspects—one related to task performance, the other to employee functioning; that **leadership styles can be learned** and must be **flexible**; and that no single style is appropriate for all situations.

Important leadership studies:
- In the **Ohio State Studies**, leadership researchers studied leadership function in terms of **initiating structures** (task orientation) and **consideration** (employee orientation), finding that no one emphasis was always effective.
- Similar **University of Michigan studies** distinguished between **job-centered** and **employee-centered approaches** to leadership and found that while employee-centered leadership was more effective, other styles could be effective and that leadership effectiveness must be judged by more than productivity.

Contingency approaches: Contingency, or **situational**, approaches to leadership stress the needs and dynamics of the particular situation and the need to adapt leadership styles to the situation. Four factors play a role in the situational approach to leadership:
- the personal characteristics of the manager
- the nature of the job itself
- the nature of the organization
- the characteristics of subordinates

Fiedler's Contingency Model: Fred E. Fiedler formulated a model in which **task structure** (structured or unstructured), **leader-member relations** (rated as poor or good), and **leader position power** (strong or weak) are situational variables that can be used to predict which type of leadership style would be most effective. Leadership style is described in terms of **least preferred coworker (LPC)** variable in which a low LPC score indicates task orientation and a high LPC score (indicating high manager effectiveness with workers) indicates employee orientation.

Path-Goal Theory: Focuses on the leader as a source of **rewards** and holds that workers can be motivated on a **path** to achieving goals if they expect that the task can be completed **(expectancy)**, think that the rewards offered are suitable **(instrumentality)** and meaningful **(valence)**.

Key 34 The managerial grid and leadership styles

OVERVIEW *The Managerial Grid is a widely used management tool that relates the two major concerns of management—people and production—in a matrix, or grid. Managers are classified by their emphasis on people and/or production, the ideal being equal emphasis on each to develop committed workforce leading to both high production and high personal satisfaction.*

Laissez-faire management: At the lower left corner of the grid is the management style characterized by minimal concern for people and minimal concern for production. Such managers pass along orders and lack initiative. This style is sometimes known as **impoverished management**.

Country club management: At the upper left of the grid (position 1,9) are managers who show a high concern for people but give little attention to production.

Task management: At the lower right of the grid (position 9,1) is the management style characterized by high concern for production and low concern for people. Such managers typically set high production quotas for their subordinates.

Middle-of-the-road management: In the middle of the grid (5,5) is the management style characterized by an adequate concern for both people and production and an attempt to balance the two.

Democratic (team) management: At the upper right of the grid (position 9,9), is what the developers of the grid, Blake and Mouton, thought was the ideal—namely, high concern for both people and production.

KEY DIAGRAM

The Blake-Mouton Managerial Grid.

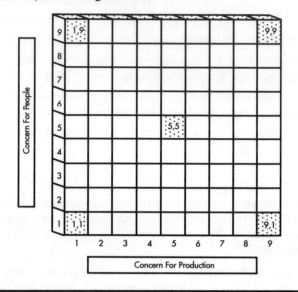

Theme 8 CONTROLLING

*C*ontrolling is the process by which a manager makes sure that the objectives and goals of the organization are met. It is one of the five major functions of management. Controlling involves setting standards, measuring performance against these standards, and taking action to correct weaknesses and improve the realization of the organization's goals. Controls are financial, usually in the form of various types of budgets and audits, and behavioral, in the form of appraisals of subordinates' performance. An ongoing activity, control is exerted at both lower and higher management levels.

Key 35 The control process: Setting standards and evaluating performance

OVERVIEW *Through control processes, managers ensure that the actual actions and functions of the organization conform to and further the organization's planned goals. Specific control processes differ in different organizations, but all involve setting standards, measuring achievement, and taking corrective action.*

Setting standards: Performance standards must be specific, concrete, and measurable in some way as well as fair and reasonable, considering past performance. As such, they enable management to determine its relative success or failure and compare its performance with that of other similar organizations or with that which occurred in the past.

Measuring standards: Performance toward a goal or standard can be measured in either **quantitative or qualitative ways**, depending on the nature of the product. When and how often in the phases of a company's operation a measurement is to be made must also be determined. Cost effectiveness and the nature of the product or company (Does the company function in a climate of rapid technological change? Does the product or service provided affect health and safety in a significant way? Or does the company operate in a stable environment?) are important factors in determining the **timing and frequency of measurement**.

Feedback: The measurement results compared with the performance standards, or goals, provide useful information about the strengths and weaknesses of an organization. Managers must then use this information, deciding whether **corrective actions** are necessary or whether present processes and standards are still the best. (Should performance standards be set higher? or lower?) Such feedback helps ensure that future planning will be effective and productive.

Key 36 Phases of control

OVERVIEW *Control processes operate at all stages, or phases, of an operation, from planning or input through process activities to the final finished, or output, stages.*

Input controls: Controls that operate before an activity begins and organizational resources are fully committed to it are known as input controls. Common in out controls are budgets, work schedules, and production and operations techniques. Also known as **steering controls**, controls at this level may require immediate corrective action to steer processes onto the correct track.

Process controls: Controls exerted while an activity is ongoing, such as performance appraisals and quality checks, are known as process controls. Such a yes/no control acts as a check on steering controls and either permits a process to continue or stops it and initiates corrective action before allowing it to continue.

Output controls: Operate after an activity or production process has been completed, often after the activity but before delivery to a customer. Output controls include quality control of a final product and audits. They evaluate an entire process and the results can be used in planning for the next work period (usually a budget period).

Key 37 Financial controls: Budgets

OVERVIEW *A **budget** is one type of financial control in an organization. It is a formal written statement of how the financial resources will be allocated to carry out the goals of the organization within a specified period of time. Probably the most widely used control, budgets may indicate revenues, costs, or profits for a specified budget period. Different types of budgets are possible, but all establish clear standards in monetary terms.*

Budgeting process: Budgets may be prepared by top management, aware of the overall financial status of the organization, and passed down to lower level managers to carry out in a process known as **top-down budgeting**. Or budgets may be prepared by lower-level managers, familiar with the day-to-day needs and operations of the various units in the organization, and then submitted to higher management for approval in a process known as **bottom-up budgeting**.

Fixed operating budgets: Operating budgets concern the operations of an organization, generally indicating the goods and services, in quantities and costs, that a company expects to use.
- A **cost, or expense, operating budget** focuses on the costs and expenses (e.g., raw materials, labor costs, overhead, administrative, accounting, and legal expenses) that a company expects to have in a budget period.
- A **revenue operating budget** focuses on projected revenue, or income, alone.
- A **profit budget** takes into account both revenue (income) and costs (expenses) to concentrate on profits.

Fixed financial budgets: Financial budgets integrate the financial planning of an organization with its operating budgets to verify the feasibility of the operating budget and to determine what financial actions need to be taken based on operational plans.

Types of fixed financial budgets:
- **Cash budget** links projected revenues and expenditures to determine **cash flow** in an organization. Then the need for short-term borrowing or the possibility of capital expenditure or investment can be explored.

- **Capital expenditure budget** indicates the projected investment in new resources for the organization (buildings, machinery, etc.).
- **Materials budget** includes an organization's **direct cost factors**, such as raw materials and labor, that are needed to allow the production of a final product.
- **Balance sheet budget** also called a **pro forma balance sheet**, links all other types of budgets into one master budget that functions as a final check on organizational activities and shows overall organizational **assets**, **liabilities**, and **equity**.

Flexible budgets: Also known as **variable** or **sliding-scale budgets**, flexible budgets consider the possibility of changing conditions and how they might affect budget items.

Key 38   Financial controls: Audits

OVERVIEW   *An audit is a formal evaluation of an organization's financial statements, performed either by an outside accounting firm or by an internal audit department. An audit can also be performed on the operation of the organization and the effectiveness of its management.*

External financial audit: Usually performed by an outside accounting firm, a firm of certified public accountants (CPAs), an external audit verifies that the company has accurately prepared its financial statements and has valued its assets and liabilities in accordance with generally accepted accounting principles. It provides assurance to bankers and potential investors of the accuracy and honesty of financial statements.

Internal financial audit: An internal audit, performed by people within the company, also verifies the accuracy of financial records and accounting procedures but usually probes into the organization's operation in greater depth. It serves as a useful tool for management in planning and decision making.

Management audit: A review of an organization's goals and the status of the plans operating to achieve these goals is accomplished through a management audit, which can be conducted by people within the organization or by outside consultants.

Key 39 Behavioral controls:
Performance appraisals

OVERVIEW *A performance appraisal is a formal evaluation of a subordinate's behavior as it relates to job-related factors. Basically a comparison between the results achieved and the performance standards set, performance appraisals allow managers to see the strengths and weaknesses of employees, the status of the organization and the needs for the future.*

Method: Performance appraisal is a continual process of providing employees with **feedback** on how they are performing their tasks for the organization. It may be informal, as in day-to-day manager comments to a subordinate, or it may be formal in a periodic written essay, ranking, or incident log that may be used in making decisions about promotions, raises, and other factors.

Essay appraisals: In an essay appraisal, a manager prepares a written summary of a subordinate's performance in terms of productivity, work attitudes, quality of work, particular strengths, weaknesses, etc.

Critical incident log: Sometimes a part of a manager's **development file** on a subordinate, a critical incident log is a record of specific employee actions that the manager considers critical examples of either good or bad performance.

Rating scale: A rating of poor to excellent is given for each subordinate in several job-related factors, such as attendance, productivity, work quality.

Employee ranking methods: A manager ranks employees in terms of their job performance. No documentation is usually given and manager bias can creep into this system. Two major forms are:
- **forced distribution ranking**, in which a predetermined percentage of workers will be ranked outstanding or unacceptable, and
- **alternation ranking**, in which a manager first ranks the best and the worst and then proceeds through a list of employees alternating ranking the next best or the next worst.

Theme 9 DECISION MAKING

Decision making is the process through which a specific action is selected as the solution to a specific problem. It is a skill that all managers must acquire. Decision making can be approached from several different ways of thinking at different levels in an organization, but most, if not all, decision making involves a careful step-by-step approach and an attempt to predict the likely outcome of the decision.

INDIVIDUAL KEYS IN THIS THEME

Key 40   Levels and types of decision making

OVERVIEW   *All managers, no matter what their level in the organizational structure, must make decisions. Each manager brings to the decision-making process a particular way of thinking and a style of approaching problems that, together with the nature of the problem, influences the type of decision made.*

Levels of decision making: Closely related to the levels of planning in an organization:
- **Strategic decision making:** Usually carried out by top management, involves the organization's overall goals and strategy, direction, and relationship with the external environment. The decisions are usually conceptual in nature, apply to the total organization, and generally have long-term consequences.
- **Administrative, or mid-level, decision making:** Administrative, or tactical, decision making, usually performed by middle-level managers, is somewhat more specific than strategic decision making and usually applies to one or a group of related departments in an organization.
- **Operational decision making:** Carried out by lower level managers (supervisors), operational decisions are specific, concern day-to-day operations, usually apply to one department or group, and have only short-term consequences.

Types of decisions: There are two major types of decisions:
- **Programmed decisions** deal with problems that are well understood, recurrent, and routine. These decisions are usually based on rule and procedures, and each time the decision is made, the process is similar. Although limiting in a way, programmed decisions can also be liberating, freeing a manager to devote time to unstructured, nonrepetitive, nonroutine matters.
- **Nonprogrammed decisions** deal with problems that are unique or unusual, not lending themselves to a predetermined procedure, rely heavily on the manager's ability, and should involve careful use of a step-by-step problem solving methodology.

Types of decision makers:

- One style of problem solving is reflected by the manager who seeks to maintain the status quo, prevent changes, and avoid or smooth over problems—the **problem avoider**.
- Another style, the most common style of managerial decision making, is that of the **problem solver**, who confronts a problem, reacts to it, and makes those changes necessary to solve it.
- Yet another style is that of the **problem seeker**, one who actively looks at situations, searching for problems or anticipating possible problems so that corrective action can be taken before the problem grows. This style focuses on the future of the organization and on planning to prevent problems.

Key 41   Steps in the decision-making process

OVERVIEW   *Although the type of thinking and style and level of decision making differ among organizations, certain basic steps characterize the decision-making process, similar to those discussed under Planning. (See Theme 4.)*

Identify the problem: A problem is something that keeps an organization from reaching its goals. A problem can be identified by studying the current situation—what is—and viewing it in terms of the organization's goals or future—what should be. If there is a gap between what is and what should be, a problem exists. (See also Key 18, Gap Analysis.) An outside consultant may be best suited to analyzing the current conditions because a manager may have a vested interest in the status quo.

Determine objectives: Once a problem has been identified, managers must decide on possible solutions and develop standards to evaluate them. Factors related to the objectives should be studied, information gathered and analyzed; and priorities set.

Develop alternatives: Once a problem and its possible solution have been identified, managers must develop several alternatives to accomplish the solution. All alternatives should be developed before any are evaluated and discarded.

Evaluate alternatives and select a plan: Each alternative should be studied in terms of how realistic it is in terms of the goals and resources of the organization, how effective it would be in solving the particular problem, and what consequences it will have on the entire organization.

Implementation: Once an alternative has been selected, it must be implemented, preferably on a pilot basis. Pilot testing is a small-scale plan on the basis of which valuable information may be gained and then applied to the full implementation.

Control and follow up: The manager measures the results of the enacted plan, using the standards set in the objectives, to determine whether the objectives have been met.

Key 42 Predicting the results
of decisions

OVERVIEW *In virtually every decision-making situation, there are some factors or variables that are uncertain or unknowable. However, the degree of uncertainty can vary greatly—and with that the chance of predicting the outcome of decisions.*

Conditions of certainty: When managers have reliable, accurate, complete, and measurable information on which to base a decision, they are operating under conditions of certainty and know what the results of the decision will be. The chance of failure is minimal under conditions of certainty, but such conditions do not occur often.

Conditions of risk: When operating under conditions of risk, the manager does not have complete information and does not know exactly what the outcome will be but does know that the outcome will probably be within a certain range of likely results. In other words, the manager under conditions of risk knows the **probability** of each possible outcome.

Conditions of uncertainty: Under conditions of uncertainty, managers make decisions without knowing the results, the probability of certain results occurring, or even what the possible results may be. Very little is known, and the possibility of failure is greatest.

Theme 10 COMMUNICATION SKILLS

*C*ommunication is the process that makes it possible for managers to carry out their responsibilities. Information must be communicated to managers, and managers must communicate with both their superiors and their subordinates. An understanding of the communication process, of the factors that affect effective communication, and of the way in which communication functions in an organization is absolutely essential for every manager. Without highly developed communication skills, a manager cannot be effective.

INDIVIDUAL KEYS IN THIS THEME
43   Model for the communication process
44   Factors affecting communication
45   Levels of communication in an organization

Key 43 Model for the communication process

OVERVIEW *Although the essential parts of the communication process are a sender, a message, and a receiver, the process itself is much more complex. It involves the way the sender expresses the content of the message, the way the message is transmitted, the way the message is interpreted and understood by the receiver, and any background factors that may affect the process.*

Sender: The person who is asking for information or wishes to pass information on to others.

Message: The information (content) that the sender wishes to transmit to another person. The content may be expressed through any of several mediums.

Encoding: The process by which the sender transmits the content. After deciding what is to be communicated, the manager must decide **how** to communicate it. The medium, or channel, selected must be appropriate to the content. *Example:* An informal postcard or short memo is not an appropriate way to explain new insurance benefits.

Channel, or Medium: The way the message is transmitted. It is sometimes impossible to separate the content from its medium. A message may be written, spoken (oral), visual (a sign or symbol), tactile (Braille), or even olfactory (the smell of baking bread to encourage bread sales). A manager must choose a medium appropriate to the content and to the people receiving the message.

Receiver: The person or persons to whom the message is sent or addressed. Without a receiver, there is no communication.

Decoding (Interpreting): The process by which the receiver interprets the message and translates it into personally meaningful information. Interpretation is affected by past experience, personal bias, and expectations.

Feedback: A reaction to the sender's message is expressed. The reverse of the original communication process, feedback has the same steps, and allows managers to know that their message has been understood.

Key 44 Factors affecting
communication

OVERVIEW *Effective communication is affected by many factors, some interpersonal, some a function of the message itself, and some related to the organizational structure.*

Number of messages: Too many messages conveyed at one time compete with one another and are generally not well understood or effective. Managers should send messages in **order of importance or priority** and avoid too much (as well as too little) communication.

Complexity A complex message with several interrelated parts is difficult to understand and act on. Managers should simplify messages and break complex messages into several separate, simple messages, each indicating its relationship to other parts of the overall message.

Filtering: The process by which a message's content is modified in some way by the character or personality of the sender or receiver. Personal prejudice, bias, and other psychological factors play important roles in message filtering.

Noise: Anything that interferes with, confuses, or distorts the communication process. The term is usually used for outside factors and includes such factors as loud music interfering with conversation or an unclear printed page.

Personal barriers: Problems in communication often arise from personal characteristics of the sender and/or receiver. *Examples:* Inattention, or tuning out, by the receiver; a lack of common vocabulary between the sender and receiver; jumping to conclusions on the part of the receiver; evaluating the sender and not the message itself; nonverbal signals that are inconsistent with the verbal message; rationalization to justify behavior; and denial, refusing to acknowledge the meaning of a message for personal reasons.

Guidelines for effective communication:
- Messages should be simple and concise and expressed in a vocabulary common to both sender and receiver.
- The manager should show a sensitivity to the receiver's framework and be aware of nonverbal as well as verbal clues.
- Two-way, face-to-face, communication is often most effective.

Key 45 Levels of communication
in an organization

OVERVIEW *Communication occurs throughout all levels of an organization, both in formal ways,—vertically, horizontally, and diagonally through the organizational chain of command—and in informal ways.*

Downward communication: High-level managers provide information about an organization's goals, and advise, instruct, and evaluate lower level managers. The managers must be sure that an adequate amount of information is passed along, that it is not filtered or modified as it is passed along down the chain of command, and that a vocabulary common to all levels is used.

Upward communication: Subordinates or lower-level managers pass information (as in progress reports and explanations), offer suggestions, and raise questions to higher-level managers. Middle-level managers should be sure that all information that may be essential, even if it is unfavorable, is passed on to higher management.

Lateral and diagonal communication: Within an organization, such communication spreads news quickly, links groups that otherwise might not communicate easily, and facilitates the use of special experience or expertise throughout an organization. It can, however, be disruptive since it does not follow the chain of command.
- **Lateral communication** occurs between individuals in a work group, between groups in a department, between departments, and between line managers and advisers (staff).
- **Diagonal communication** occurs between one department at one level in the organization's hierarchy and another department at a different level.

Informal communication—grapevine: In every organization, there exists informal, unstructured communication—a *grapevine,* and managers must recognize its existence and the role it sometimes plays in organizational functioning.

Theme 11   WORK GROUP DYNAMICS

*G*roups of different types arise, develop, establish standards, and carry out their functions in all organizations. In fact, an organization may be viewed as a large group or group of groups. Therefore, an understanding of basic group dynamics, characteristics and norms, and the managerial implications of these factors is essential for all managers.

Key 46   Types of groups

OVERVIEW   *A group is two or more people who work together and interact for a common purpose. Within an organization, formal and informal groups exist, each with its specific purpose.*

Formal groups: Designated by the organization itself, usually for a specific purpose, and given the authority to accomplish its task.
- **Command group:** Also known as a **functional group**, made up of a manager and subordinates and following the hierarchical structure of the organization.
- **Task group:** Set up by the organization to complete a specific project or task, usually within a specified period of time. Members are chosen for particular knowledge or expertise, and the hierarchical structure of the group may not follow that of the organization as a whole. *Examples:* Project teams, matrix groups (see Theme 5), and committees.

Informal groups: Not designated by the organization and may form whenever people with similar interests interact. A leader, if there is one, emerges by force of personality and the interests of the group. Although not formed by the organization, informal groups may affect and be affected by the organization.
- **Interest group:** Individuals with a common work interest (e.g., plant safety) may form an interest group; it usually continues only as long as the particular interest or concern.
- **Friendship (peer) group:** Individuals with a common outside interest (e.g., bowling, softball, golf) may form an informal group that may extend through many levels of the organization. An organization can discourage such groups by setting up conflicting schedules for members or encourage such groups, through sponsorship of a team.

Committees: A formal group set up by the organization, a committee is really a type of task (or project) group. (See Key 26.) Because it has a greater knowledge base than any one individual and because extreme opinions are usually filtered out, in theory a committee can make a better decision than any individual member. A committee is effective if it has cooperative, hardworking, knowledgeable members led by a strong and skilled chairperson who encourages participation but keeps the group focused on a well-defined goal.

Key 47 Groups: Their development and characteristics

OVERVIEW *Groups are more complex than the sum of the actions of members working on a common goal. Groups have an identity of their own; evolve through various stages of development; and establish standards members are expected to follow. A cohesive group then functions efficiently and creatively.*

Group evolution: After a group has been formed and charged with its task, members must get to know one another and each individual's skills and expertise so that acceptance and confidence grow. As **cohesiveness** develops, a **group identity** forms, participation and leadership styles emerge, and the group attempts to understand the exact nature of its task. Problem solving, evaluation of ideas, and decision making follow as members work cooperatively, not competitively, and become efficient. The mature group then takes on its final form—with expected behavior, or group norms.

Group norms: Within each group, a range of behavior is considered acceptable and desirable—the group norm. Those performing above (a "rate buster") or below the norm are subject to peer pressure. Group norms lead to a high level of conformity and may stifle initiative.

Group status: Individuals will not enthusiastically participate in a group if no status is attached to the group. Group status depends on the status of individual members, the nature of the task assigned, the success, and the rewards the group may achieve.

Group size: There is no ideal size. The group must be small enough to allow members to get to know one another, feel a sense of commitment to the group and task, and communicate effectively, yet large enough to include those skills necessary for the task. The leader's effective span of control must also be considered.

Generation of ideas: Groups are frequently required to develop creative ideas to solve problems or improve conditions. Techniques developed for this process include:
* **brainstorming**, in which group members express ideas (alternatives) that are not evaluated until all ideas have been proposed

- the **Delphi technique**, in which group members answer questions anonymously and then evaluate summaries of all group members' answers
- the **nominal group technique**, in which each member of a group writes down as many possible solutions to a problem as he or she can think of. Recorded ideas are then discussed and ranked for submission to management.

Key 48 Groups and management

OVERVIEW *Groups are found in all organizations, and to be effective, a manager must understand how groups relate to one another in the organization and how managers act in controlling a group and relating it to other groups.*

Micro vs. macro views of an organization: Management may view the group nature of an organization in either of two ways.
- In the **macroscopic view**, the organization is viewed as one large group.
- In the **microscopic view**, the organization is viewed as a collection of several small interrelated groups with employee actions taking place within and between subgroups.

Likert's Linkpin View: In the **microscopic view** held by Rensis Likert, each manager of a group serves as a **linking pin between groups**. Managers belong to command (functional, hierarchical) groups within an organization that includes themselves and their subordinates. At the same time, each manager belongs to another group made up of other managers at that level and their immediate mutual superior, a higher level manager. To be effective, management must understand how the manager of each group links the group to other groups in the organization.

Span of control: Span of control is the number of subordinates a manager can effectively control. It depends on the skills of the manager, the nature of the job, the overall organizational structure, and the type of employees supervised.
- The narrower the span of control the more direct supervision, the more managers needed, and the higher the costs—a so-called **tall organization**.
- The wider the span, the less supervision and the more responsibility on subordinates—a so-called **flat organization**.

Key 49   Quality circles

OVERVIEW *One specific way in which a formal group and management work together on questions of mutual interest is through a Quality Circle (QC). However, a QC can only succeed—for both workers and the organization— if certain conditions are present.*

Quality Circle: A group established by management (a formal group) made up of eight or ten workers and management representatives that **meets on company time**, usually once a week, to address problems of **quality control**, **efficiency**, and **productivity**.

Prerequisites for QC success: To be effective a quality circle must have the **full support of management** who are willing to allow the group to meet during work hours (at the risk of lost productivity) and give it the authority to identify problems and make suggestions. **Unions** must also **support** the group and be assured that no matters proper to collective bargaining or union negotiations will be raised. In addition, all QC members must be **trained in problem-solving skills**.

Potential benefit to management:
- Increased productivity and efficiency
- Improved product quality
- A climate of worker-management cooperation

Potential benefit to workers:
- Worker members of a quality circle may receive a cash reward, often a percentage of the savings realized through their recommendations.
- Membership in the QC may be considered a factor in promotions.
- All workers may benefit from a climate of worker-management cooperation.

Theme 12 MOTIVATION

*T*he ability to motivate people is a skill that all managers must acquire. Without it, they cannot accomplish their goals—and the goals of the organization. Several theories of motivation have been developed throughout the years, but surprisingly, a general agreement about the overall factors that motivate people of all levels has emerged.

Key 50 Motivating factors

OVERVIEW *People must be motivated to accomplish their personal goals and the goals of the organization of which they are part. Although individual motives may be affected by external circumstances and stage in life, the motives, or basic needs, of most people are remarkably similar.*

Motivation: The process of stimulating an individual to take action that will accomplish a desired goal, an important skill for all involved in management, defined as working with and through other people (motivating other people) to accomplish the goals of the organization and its members.

Motivation process: Unfulfilled needs create **tension**. This tension produces a **motive** that causes actions and **behavior** that is aimed at satisfying the need in order to reduce the tension.

KEY DIAGRAM

Motive		Behavior		Human Need
(tension)		(activity)		(tension reduction)
e.g., desire to succeed		study, learn		self-fulfillment

Motivating factors: In studies, people—be they high-level executives, middle-level managers, or secretaries and office clerks—name the same motivating factors. The factors given most often include:
- Respect for me as a person
- Good pay
- Opportunity for self-development and improvement
- Feeling my job is important
- Opportunity to do interesting work
- Large amount of freedom on the job

Factors affecting motivation: Various factors affect an individual's motivation at different **stages in life**. Factors like good pay and chance for promotion may motivate a young person with a family to support more than they will motivate a 55-year-old. **External factors**, such as the overall economic status of the nation, also affect personal motivation. *Example:* Job security becomes important in times of economic slump.

Key 51   Early theories of motivation

OVERVIEW   *An understanding of early theories of motivation can be useful to managers as they try to motivate their subordinates. Two of the earliest theories—Maslow's Needs Theory and Herzberg's Motivation-Hygiene Theory—focused on needs and factors still considered in modern theories.*

Traditional theory of motivation: Evolved in the early 20th century from the scientific management theory. It held that **money** is the prime motivating factor and that financial rewards should be related directly to performance.

Maslow's Hierarchy of Needs theory: As the Human Relations movement grew, more attention was focused on the worker. Abraham Maslow held that individual unsatisfied needs are the main source of motivation. He placed **five needs in a hierarchy** from most basic to most mature:
- Basic, or physiological (as needed for survival)
- Safety
- A sense of belonging
- Ego status
- Self-actualization.

Sequence: Maslow believed that an individual must satisfy one need before feeling free to take on the tensions associated with the next level and before trying new behaviors aimed at satisfying the next higher need.

Herzberg's Motivation-Hygiene theory: Focusing more specifically on the work situation, Frederick I. Herzberg believed that only those needs that corresponded to Maslow's ego status and self-actualization levels were direct sources of work motivation. He called these factors **motivators**. He thought that the lower level needs of survival and safety, which he labelled **dissatisfiers**, or **maintenance factors**, centered on issues not directly related to work and were factors that most people assumed would be met. A sense of belonging, he found, overlapped both categories.

Maintenance factors: Among Herzberg's maintenance (dissatisfier) factors were salary, job security, and good working conditions.

Motivating factors: Among his motivating factors were the challenge of the job itself, achievement, recognition, responsibility, advancement, and growth.

KEY DIAGRAM

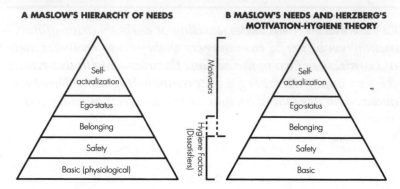

A MASLOW'S HIERARCHY OF NEEDS

- Self-actualization
- Ego-status
- Belonging
- Safety
- Basic (physiological)

B MASLOW'S NEEDS AND HERZBERG'S MOTIVATION-HYGIENE THEORY

Motivators

Hygiene Factors (Dissatisfiers)

- Self-actualization
- Ego-status
- Belonging
- Safety
- Basic

Needs and motives. A shows Maslow's Hierarchy of Needs Theory. B shows the relationship of Maslow's theory and that of Herzberg, who focused on motives as they relate to the workplace. As you can see, Herzberg thought that the upper-level needs identified by Maslow served to motivate work performance, that lower-level, or basic, needs acted as maintenance factors, possibly dissatisfiers; and that the need to belong could function as either a motivating or dissatisfying factor.

Key 52   Other theories of motivation

OVERVIEW   *Advances in understanding human nature and the evolution of management theory have led to the rise of several theories of motivation. Familiarity with these theories is important to managers as they attempt to influence and motivate subordinates.*

McClelland's theory of human motives: According to David McClelland, three basic motives or needs—**achievement**, **power**, and **affiliation**—affect behavior in the workplace. Motives of achievement (entrepreneurship) and power (managerial success) are positive factors, leading to high performance, while affiliation motivation is negative, tending to interfere with performance and objectivity.

Reinforcement theory: Based on the ideas of psychologist B.F. Skinner, reinforcement theory holds that **reinforced behavior will be repeated** and that nonreinforced behavior will not be repeated. In other words, the consequences that people experience for a certain specific behavior determine their level of motivation.

Expectancy theory: Victor Vroom developed a theory of motivation focusing on an individual's goals and expectation of attaining them. The theory holds that individuals can determine the outcomes they prefer and estimate the chances of obtaining them. Also known as the **preference-expectancy theory**, it stresses that organizations must relate rewards to performance and be sure that the rewards are those wanted by the recipients.

Equity theory: According to Stacy Adams, an exponent of equity theory, the **perception of unfairness** is a powerful motivating factor in business. It depends on a comparison of perceived equity of pay and rewards among employees and comparison of compensation based on factors such as education, experience, and seniority.

McGregor's Theory X and Theory Y: Douglas McGregor contributed to the Behavioral School of Management through his Theory X and Theory Y, much of which is applicable to motivation. (See Key 6.)

Theme 13 MANAGING CHANGE AND CONFLICT IN AN ORGANIZATION

*N*o viable organization is static. Changes occur in all organizations and conflicts develop at all levels. All managers must develop skill in dealing with change and conflict, recognizing their important roles in an organization and learning how to manage them to minimize their drawbacks and maximize their positive effects in stimulating creativity and growth. In other words, a manager must develop the skill to make change and conflict work for an organization, not against it.

INDIVIDUAL KEYS IN THIS THEME

53 Change: Its role and climate

54 Strategy for implementing change

55 Conflict: Its role and sources in an organization

56 Managing conflict in an organization

Key 53 Change: Its role
and climate

OVERVIEW *No organization exists in a vacuum. Internal and external forces stimulate change in an organization and help create a future-oriented continuum and climate for growth.*

Change: The process by which the way an individual or organization acts is transformed from one set of behaviors to another. Change occurs daily in an organization—either by design, spontaneously, or by default.

Organizational climate: The overall political, social, and economic environment of an organization. It is affected by external forces, the power structure within the organization, and the needs of and demands on the organization.

External forces for change: Factors outside the organization itself often force change. Among these factors are changes in the desires and spending habits of consumers; changes in the pricing structure of competitors; new governmental regulations; and advances in technology leading to new products or new methods.

Internal forces for change: Factors operating within an organization can also trigger change. Among these are budgetary demands; changes in the reward system; changes in stockholder wishes and other changes in the overall financial picture of the company; and any other changes in the overall power (hierarchical) structure of the organization and its human resources.

Change as a continuum: Change is oriented to the **future**. Each individual change provokes a reaction. That leads to another change, creating a chain effect of changes oriented to the future. **No one change is final**.

The role of change: The organization that does not change usually is doomed to failure because it cannot meet the changing needs and opportunities of the environment. Thus, although **change is difficult** and there is a **resistance to change** among individuals and groups, it is necessary for the success and growth of an organization.

Key 54   Strategy for implementing change

OVERVIEW   *Change is difficult and is best implemented through a careful and detailed process that considers alternatives and their consequences and allows subordinates to participate in the process in a meaningful way.*

Recognize need for change: Either external or internal events may stimulate a need for change, sometimes referred to as a **perceived need**. This need can be a sense that ''something'' needs to be changed or improved to make the organization more **efficient** (doing things correctly) and **effective** (doing the correct thing). The need for change may focus on any aspect of the business.

Diagnose problem: The scope or extent of the problem is identified; the problem is clearly defined; symptoms are separated from the problem itself; the desired outcome is stated; and the ways by which the outcome can be evaluated (measured) are determined.

Develop alternatives: Through brainstorming or other techniques for generating ideas, several possible solutions to the problem should be developed.

Analyze alternatives and select one: Each proposed solution must be evaluated in terms of the organization's people, structure, and environment as well as in terms of potential costs and anticipated benefits. Each alternative becomes more or less attractive depending on its constraints and probability for success. The decision may be made formally, as is often the case with major changes, or informally. A lack of a decision is a decision to continue ''business as usual.''

Implement the decision: Management may implement a change in an **autocratic way**, ignoring the natural resistance to change, the need to undo current behavior patterns, and the tendency to do ''business as usual.'' Or, management may take a **participative approach**, involving subordinates in developing and implementing the change. If subordinates are willing, this approach, which allows subordinates to **''buy into''** the problem and its solution, is often successful.

Evaluate the results: Evaluation allows management to know whether the change worked and the planned outcome was achieved. It also provides feedback to be used in future planning.

Key 55 Conflict: Its role and sources in an organization

OVERVIEW *Conflict within an organization is a disagreement between two or more organization members or groups. Conflict is always present in an organization, and it plays an important role.*

Role of conflict: Conflict, basically a dispute over how to achieve an organization's goals, is not necessarily bad for an organization. It can lead to increased creativity and the introduction of changes and innovations. However, it can also sap organizational energy, weaken focus, and waste managers' time. To benefit from conflict, managers must recognize it as a **constant force** and deal with it constructively.

Levels of conflict: Conflict may exist **between organizations** (they compete in the marketplace); **between departments or groups** (they compete for organizational resources or have different perspectives); **between an individual and a group** (the individual may not conform to group norms); and **between individuals** (they may have different functions or perspectives or personalities that clash). Conflict can also occur **within an individual** (he or she may need to decide between undesirable alternatives or equally good methods).

Sources of conflict: There are several basic sources of conflict in an organization. Chief among these are:

- **Competition for organizational resources**. *Example:* Money, raw materials, personnel.
- **Differences in goals and perspectives**. *Example:* Different departments have different immediate objectives; some may have long-term perspectives, while others want short-term results.
- **Situations in which work activities of one department depend on the completion of activities by another department**.
- **Failures in the communication process** leading to a lack of information or misinformation.
- The **organizational framework itself**. *Example:* Conflict between line and staff employees.

Change—a source of conflict: Change of any kind often leads to conflict. One technique to handle change, known as **organizational development (OD)**, uses **case studies** and an **eclectic approach** to try to improve an organization's **problem solving skills** and develop a **methodology** for dealing with conflict resulting from change.

Key 56 Managing conflict in an organization

OVERVIEW *To minimize the disruptive effect of conflict and to use it as a constructive force, managers should become familiar with various techniques of managing conflict. Although many of the techniques, including avoidance, smoothing over, and compromise, do not address the causes of the problem or conflict, they may, nonetheless, be effective under certain conditions.*

Avoidance: If the solution to a particular problem is not vital to the functioning of an organization and management is willing to overlook the causes of the conflict, managers may simply avoid dealing with the conflict by physically separating the conflicting parties (if their work involves no interaction) completely; by limiting their contact and watching any interactions; or by simply ignoring the fact that a conflict exists, pretending that there is no problem and/or that it will go away by itself. Avoidance saves manager time, but may lead to more severe problems later.

Dominance—forcing a resolution: Faced with conflict, managers may exert their power and autocratically impose a resolution. This method saves time and reinforces the organization's hierarchical structure, but may lead to employee resentment, and, more importantly, may not deal with the causes of the conflict. High-level managers may be better informed of the organization's overall goals, but may not have detailed knowledge of the events or circumstances leading to the conflict.

Smoothing over: Unless a manager has information that the conflicting parties do not have, this method of dealing with conflict is usually ineffective. In it, managers attempt to minimize the importance of the disagreement and to stress points of agreement between the conflicting parties so that harmony and peace are maintained. Since the causes of the problem are not addressed, they will likely come up again.

Compromise: In this method of dealing with conflict, managers attempt to find a middle ground between the disagreeing parties. Each side ''wins'' something, but neither is completely satisfied, and resentment as well as the underlying causes of the initial conflict may linger. For compromise to be effective in any way, both parties must be on the same level in the organizational hierarchy. At times, in an effort to arrive at a compromise, managers may insist on going "by the book" or may try to compensate one party for giving in and ending the conflict.

Confrontation: Unlike the other techniques, confrontation deals with the causes of the conflict. The conflicting parties are asked to express their views directly to each other in the hope of attaining mutual understanding. Then they are guided in emphasizing overall organizational goals—**superordinate goals**—over individual or group goals to resolve the conflict. Confrontation requires a great deal of a manager's time and energy and may lead to emotional outbursts and bad feelings, but it can be successful if all participants are willing to cooperate in the process.

Theme 14 EXECUTIVE SKILLS

*O*ne of the most important skills that managers—in any type of organization or at any level of management—must develop is skill in managing time. Managers must also pursue their own career plan, and to do this, skill in preparing a résumé and cover letter and in being interviewed is essential.

INDIVIDUAL KEYS IN THIS THEME	
57	Time management
58	Preparing a résumé and cover letter
59	A successful interview

Key 57   Time management

OVERVIEW   *Time is a unique and precious resource, one that must be planned and managed. A knowledge of what type of time a manager most benefits from and of ways to obtain more of it are key elements in managerial success.*

Characteristics of time: Time has five unique features—it is inelastic (the supply never increases); irreplaceable; perishable; always in short supply; and cannot be rented or bought.

Time-consuming tasks of a manager: Time is taken up by three basic types of tasks. **Boss-imposed tasks** impose on a manager's **employee time:** the manager is doing things personally, acting as an employee. **Organization-imposed** tasks take up **supervisory time:** the manager is assigning tasks to others. **Self-imposed tasks** take up **executive** and **discretionary time:** the manager is delegating authority and responsibility to others. A manager's objective should be to spend as much time as possible in the executive time category, generating more self-imposed tasks. This will not happen if the manager allows subordinates to infringe on discretionary time.

Apportioning managerial time: Moving up the organization's hierarchical chain, a manager should spend more time in managing through delegating and less in operating through doing. To state it another way, as management activities and demands increase, involvement in the technical or vocational activities of the organization should decrease. (See Key 1.)

Using time better: Better time utilization involves becoming aware of how time is really spent (keeping a time log helps) and then consolidating and managing the time. Some hints for using time better:
- Make a plan for the day.
- Set deadlines.
- Set aside time for thinking and creating.
- Concentrate on doing one thing at a time—**chunk time**. (Most important tasks require a fairly large period of time; to spend less than the minimum required is a waste of time.)
- Strike a balance between important jobs and necessary jobs.
- Take a short break every two hours.

Approaches to time management: Time management should occur in all three main areas of managerial concern: production, administration, and delegation.

- **Production:** Separate the essential from the nonessential; be persistent;, learn to work anywhere and use spare time; and don't waste time on trifles: decide trifles quickly.
- **Administration:** Schedule time; prioritize tasks and start with the number one item and complete it (doing it the correct way) before moving on to the second item.
- **Delegation:** Know which tasks can be safely delegated; figure out who can help most effectively; and let them help.

Key 58   Preparing a résumé
and cover letter

OVERVIEW   *In pursuing a career life plan, a manager must assess personal strengths and weaknesses, likes and dislikes, interests and goals before exploring the possibilities. At some point, development of a résumé and cover letter and preparation for an effective interview are called for.*

Résumé: A written summary of personal education and experience intended to demonstrate qualifications for a particular position. An effective résumé is designed with a particular type of job in mind and a clearly articulated objective substantiated by reasons an applicant is qualified for that particular type of work. A selling tool or advertisement of skills and accomplishments, it is intended to stimulate interest on the part of the potential employer in order to gain an interview and further consideration for the position.

Guidelines for résumé writing:
- Be honest. False information may be grounds for dismissal.
- Keep the résumé focused. Different résumés should be prepared, each focused on the particular type of job sought.
- Do not include personal data, such as age, marital status, or height and weight
- Be sure the résumé is well organized and brief—no more than one or two pages.
- Use light colored paper—white, sand, buff, light gray.
- Avoid gimmicks (e.g., fancy binders).
- Be sure the résumé is well typed and duplicated.
- Be sure that the résumé is free of grammar, spelling or punctuation errors.

Formats for résumés: The formats most widely used for résumés are:
- **Chronological:** The most widely used format, it lists experience (previous jobs) chronologically, starting with the most recent, and gives job title and a description of accomplishments for each job. This format is best used when there are few or no gaps in employment history.
- **Functional:** If there are gaps in employment history or numerous job changes in a given period, a functional résumé may be pref-

erable. This categorizes experience into several job functions (e.g., planning, communication, leadership), emphasizing job capabilities and deemphasizing dates, names, and places.

- **Combination:** If experience has been largely with one company, a combination résumé is best. It uses a functional format and includes job titles, company names, and dates. It emphasizes skills and abilities.

Cover letter: A cover letter is a short letter (three or four paragraphs) written to a potential employer with a résumé attached. Guidelines for writing a cover letter:

- Use printed, personal letterhead stationery, if possible.
- If responding to a newspaper ad, use some language from the ad in the cover letter.
- Include the name and title of the individual with whom you are seeking an interview, if this is possible.
- Emphasize any particular skills that meet the company's needs.
- Suggest a specific interview time.

Key 59   A successful interview

OVERVIEW   *A job interview is a face-to-face meeting between two people to explore mutual interest as it relates to a specific job. It is a structured conversation that allows the interviewer to assess the applicant's potential and the applicant to assess whether the job is attractive. An interview is an important part of the hiring process for any managerial position, and knowing how to have a winning interview is an important skill for any manager.*

Personal preparation: Dress appropriately, as you would if you were hired for that particular job in that particular company. Be on time and be prepared for possible emergencies (e.g., parking problems). Be ready to describe personal accomplishments briefly—things you want the interviewer to remember and that reinforce your suitability for the position. Become familiar with the company—what it does, its major product line, its reputation, its needs.

The interview: During the interview itself, follow these guidelines:
- Be aware of the image you are projecting (e.g., what you read while waiting, how you sit, mannerisms).
- Greet the interviewer with a firm handshake and make eye contact.
- Do not smoke.
- Be a good listener. Hear what the interviewer is saying about the person they want to hire.

Parts of an interview: An interview generally consists of four parts: the greeting, typical questions asked by the interviewer, questions the applicant asks, and the close.

Greeting: During the greeting stage, establish rapport, maintain eye contact, and be aware of the image you are projecting.

Typical interview questions: When answering questions, omit superfluous details and emphasize the benefits that you can bring to the company. Watch for nonverbal feedback and shorten your response if you notice that the interviewer's attention is wandering. If you do not know the answer to a technical question, admit it and do not panic. Try to mention your strongest points near the end of the interview. Some typical questions (and hints to consider when answering):
- Tell me about yourself. (Take the initiative. Mention your strengths and how they relate to the company.)

- What are your strengths? (Sell yourself, emphasize specific skills and knowledge of the industry.)
- Why should I hire you? (Again, sell yourself, stressing motivation, familiarity with the industry, previous successes.)
- What are your weaknesses? (Be self-confident and mention non-job-related weaknesses, or better yet, present a strength as a weakness.)
- What are your long-range goals? (Be sure that your response shows career planning, foresight, self-knowledge, realistic expectations.)
- What is important to you in a job? (Stress that you want to do a good job and contribute to the goals of the company.)

Questions the applicant may ask: It is appropriate for an applicant also to ask questions. It is generally a good idea not to discuss salary or benefits until you have been offered the job, but the following questions are appropriate:
- May I see a copy of the job description?
- To whom would I be responsible?
- With whom would I be working?
- What are the advancement opportunities?
- How much travel is involved with the position?
- What are the major markets? Biggest competitors?

The close—and after: The interviewer may offer the next step—going about the hiring procedure, coming back for another meeting, or expressing no interest. Be courteous, and thank the interviewer. (You may ask for an evaluation of the interview if you wish.) Within four days of the interview, send a short thank-you note (on personal stationery, if possible). Briefly review the major points covered in the interview, express your continuing interest, and suggest a definite timetable for an additional meeting or conversation.

Theme 15 PRODUCTION AND OPERATIONS MANAGEMENT

*A*s businesses themselves and the projects they handle have become more and more complex, the need for resource planning, scheduling techniques, controlling and coordinating methodologies, and other tools to help managers have increased. Many techniques have been developed, known collectively as production and operations management (POM). Several of the most widely used techniques are discussed in the following keys, including break-even analysis, PERT, MRP, decision tables, and economic order quantity.

Key 60 Break-even analysis

OVERVIEW *Break-even analysis is a technique that allows managers to determine the minimum sales necessary if revenues are to equal costs. Factors included in the analysis include all types of production costs, total revenue, and pricing. The technique can be expanded to estimate profits and help in deciding on capital expenditures.*

Production costs: There are three types of costs associated with production:

- **Fixed costs:** Those production costs that do not vary with the quantity produced. *Examples:* Rent, mortgage payment or other building expenses; insurance.
- **Variable costs:** Those production costs that vary directly with the quantity produced. *Examples:* Costs of raw materials necessary for production; labor costs.
- **Semivariable costs:** Those costs that vary with the quantity produced, but not in a direct way. In practice, of course, many costs are fixed or partly fixed under certain circumstances and variable under others, and it is difficult to categorize them as simply as our definition implies.

Revenue and pricing: Total revenue is equal to the price per unit sold times the quantity sold. When total revenue equals total production costs, the manufacturer breaks even, neither losing nor profiting. A calculation of total production costs—and thus of the total revenue needed to break even—can be used to determine price per unit. Another way of viewing pricing is through **contribution margin**—the amount from the sale of each unit and the paying of variable costs that is left to contribute to fixed costs.

Mathematical formula: Information on costs, pricing, and revenue can be put together in a mathematical equation that determines the break-even quantity:

$$\text{break-even quantity} = \frac{\text{fixed costs}}{\text{unit price} - \text{variable costs per unit}}$$

Calculating profit: The basic break-even analysis can be expanded to project profit. **Profit** is total revenues minus total costs. Using the factors of break-even analysis, profit can be determined by:

profit = total revenue   − total costs

      (price × quantity) − (fixed costs + [variable costs × quantity])

A knowledge of expected profit or of the changes (e.g., changes in unit pricing or in quantity produced) necessary to ensure profits can be used in making decisions about machinery purchases and other capital expenditures.

Potential problems: Break-even analysis is based on several assumptions and therein lies its limitations. For example, fixed costs may not remain fixed (e.g., rent or mortgage payments may change); variable costs per unit may not remain constant (e.g., equipment failures or bottlenecks created by rapid increases in production may lead to higher labor costs); and price per unit may not remain constant (e.g., large-scale discounters may change policies).

Key 61 Profit matrix (decision table)

OVERVIEW *A profit matrix is a tool that relates possible managerial choices, external conditions and their likelihood of occurrence, and the likely payoff of each choice to determine which choice would probably be most profitable. A* **profit matrix,** *or decision table as it is sometimes called, is a graphic tool that is widely used to help managers decide on a specific course of action when there are several possible courses of action. Factors considered are external demands, managerial alternatives, worst-case scenarios, and maximum, minimum, and most likely expected results.*

Constructing a decision table: To construct a decision table, list external demands (e.g., customer demand) horizontally across the top of a grid and managerial choices (e.g., different possible orders) down the vertical axis of the grid. Then, based on the cost of the alternatives and the revenues based on demand, calculate the payoff, or profit, for each situation.

Using a profit matrix to make a decision: Once the profit matrix is constructed, the **maximum**, **minimum**, and **average payoff** (profit) from each managerial alternative, given different possible demands, is evident. Management may take an optimistic view and decide to pursue the alternative with the best possible results, ignoring possible inferior outcomes. Or, following a "worst-case scenario," management may be pessimistic and assume that the lowest payoff is really the most likely and pursue that alternative. Or, on a safer course, management may consider both extremes unlikely and pursue the alternative that provides the **best average payoff**—an **equally likely solution**.

Key 62 Economic order quantity (EOQ)

OVERVIEW *Economic Order Quantity (EOQ) is a quantitative operations and management technique used to determine when and how much raw materials for inventory should be ordered to be most cost effective.*

Factors included in EOQ:
- Number of units of a product ordered
- Optimal (in terms of ordering and inventory costs) amount of each inventory order
- Demand for inventory units over a period of time (usually one year)
- Ordering costs—costs incurred (e.g., clerical work) in ordering
- Carrying costs—costs (e.g., storage, insurance, spoilage) incurred in maintaining the inventory

Relationship of ordering, carrying, and inventory costs: There is an **inverse relationship between ordering costs and carrying costs**. As ordering costs go up (more frequent but smaller orders) carrying costs go down (fewer units to store). **Inventory costs are the total of ordering costs and carrying costs**. Total inventory costs are lowest where ordering costs equal carrying costs.

Other factors affecting EOQ: Other factors considered in determining EOQ are **inventory usage pattern**—whether inventory use is constant and if so, at what rate per period of time—and **safety stock**,—an amount of inventory that a company desires to keep on hand for emergencies (e.g., a delay in an expected inventory delivery).

A mathematical formula: EOQ is a mathematical formula that allows a manager to determine what amount of inventory order is most cost effective. The formula for EOQ is:

$$EOQ = \sqrt{\frac{2(\text{yearly demand for inventory units} \times \text{cost per each inventory order})}{\text{cost of carrying each inventory unit for one year}}}$$

Key 63   Techniques for managing complex projects— PERT and CPM

OVERVIEW   *As manufacturing and engineering projects became more complex with numerous interrelated component subprojects, the need for systems to schedule and coordinate these projects developed. Several managerial tools have been developed to handle multi-component projects, two of the better known of which are Project Evaluation Review Technique (PERT) and Critical Path Method (CPM).*

Steps in a PERT or CPM network: In a complex project, the interrelationship of many subprojects requires a **network analysis** to see how the components are related. The typical steps in developing a PERT network are:
- Break the project down into individual component **tasks**, or **activities**.
- Determine whether the activities are simultaneous or sequential and arrange them in a logical and sequential order.
- Determine the length of time required to complete each activity.
- Diagram the activities and times in a chart.
- Determine the shortest time in which all the activities in the project can be completed.

Activities (tasks) and time: Each activity really has two important time elements—its starting time and its ending time. The starting and ending points in time are called **events**. In most PERT charts, events are represented by circles or dots, and activities are represented by arrows. An arrow (activity) is then drawn between two circles (its starting time and its ending time).

Determining sequences and simultaneous activities: To chart the activities in a PERT network, it is necessary to determine which activities have **immediate predecessors**—in other words, which activity must be completed before going on to the next, so that the ending point of one activity becomes the starting point of the next activity in sequence. Some activities may also be simultaneous and can go on at the same time. In some networks, **slack time** occurs.

Slack time is time waiting while another activity is completed that is necessary before proceeding to the next activity.

Critical path: The purpose of a PERT network is to determine the critical path, or **the shortest time in which a project with many component subprojects can be completed**. It is the longest route through a network, determined by adding the amount of time needed for each activity in the sequence. The critical path determines the total length of time, or completion date, of a project.

Value of a PERT (CPM) network: A PERT network allows a manager to see the relationship of subprojects; allows effective planning and allocation of resources where and when they are needed; facilitates the recognition of problem areas, or bottlenecks; and encourages effective planning.

Key 64   Master production schedules

OVERVIEW   *Another production and operations management tool is a Master Production Schedule (MPS) that combines Materials Requirements Planning (MRP) and Capacities Requirements Planning (CRP) into an integrated, computer-assisted approach to production.*

Materials Requirements Planning (MRP): An approach to determining the quantity and timing of inventory so that optimal production can be maintained. Once management decides on a specific production number, a MRP system enables the manager to determine the materials and time requirements needed to meet that production standard, based on a **bill of materials (BOM)**, or product structure, which details the materials needed for each unit of production.

Capacities Requirements Planning (CRP): In CRP, the planned production is converted into standard **hours of load**, which, applied to human resources and machinery, shows how much time is needed to accomplish the planned production. Using CRP, the manager can analyze the inventory and production resources of the company to help determine a production schedule based on **available load**.

Master Production Schedule (MPS): A computer-based program that combines an MRP and a CRP. Time and material requirements are combined with the inventory and production capabilities of the company to produce a master schedule, or approach to production.

Key 65 Other POM techniques

OVERVIEW *There are several other production and operations management techniques, many of which use advanced computer technology. All are decision-making tools designed to help managers allocate resources, determine the effect of variables on a situation, and decide on the best course of action to maximize productivity. Three widely used techniques are: Simulation Modeling, Decision Trees, and Linear Programming.*

Simulations: In this technique, a **model,** or simulation, of a real-world situation—an organization or part of an organization—is constructed to determine what will happen as time passes or as certain variables change.
- With the use of computers, simulation models can be speeded up so what is likely to occur in several years can be indicated (or seen on the computer screen) within a few seconds.
- Simulations also allow experimenting with different variables without interfering with real organization operations.
- Simulation modeling is best suited to very complex problems (e.g., astronaut training).

Decision trees: Another widely used POM technique, a decision tree is a visual representation of steps in the decision-making process. Alternatives are represented as branches from a choice fork. The end of each branch further branches off, showing the outcomes of that alternative. Costs and probabilities of occurrence are added to the tree as well as other information. The information is put together and the tree pruned for a decision.

Linear programming: A POM technique that takes advantage of advanced computer technology, linear programming is best suited to problems that can be expressed in directly proportional relationships (linear). The technique is used to determine the optimal allocation of resources to achieve the desired end.

Theme 16 MANAGEMENT INFORMATION SYSTEMS

A Management Information System (MIS) is a widely used, computerized system for managing information—the key to all managerial success. It is a formal system for making available to management timely and accurate information necessary for decision making and effective planning, operation, and control. This system is one of the many systems that have been developed to handle specific aspects of the increasingly complex world of management.

INDIVIDUAL KEYS IN THIS THEME

Key 66 Importance of information

OVERVIEW *The possession of accurate and timely information is essential for all managers. Without it, they cannot make effective decisions and help lead their companies to increased productivity and market success.*

Value of information: Information has two important values or roles to play in an organization.
- First, it is necessary for and can improve managerial **decision-making**. Decisions are only as good as the information on which they are based, so information is key to decision-making.
- Second, information can give its possessor a **competitive advantage in the marketplace**. As such, information becomes a **weapon**, and management has the responsibility to acquire, use, and safeguard information.

Information requirements: Different level managers have different information needs. The value of an MIS is that it can provide the required information to the people who need it.
- High-level executives need broad-based information for use in their strategic planning for the organization.
- Lower-level managers or unit supervisors need detailed information on day-to-day operations.

Usefulness of information: Information must be **appropriate to the task** (detailed information for a first-line manager, broad general information for a corporate executive). Information must also be **complete** and **accurate**. And, it must also be **timely**; if the information is not available when it is needed, it no longer has much value.

Information is flexible: The tremendous increase in the amount of knowledge in the twentieth century and the ability, with advanced computer systems, to generate, manipulate, synthesize, and evaluate data, has led to a realization that information must be accessible in many forms.

Key 67 MIS subsystems

OVERVIEW *An MIS has several subsystems designed to provide a particular type of information or handle information in a specific way to aid in the decision-making process.*

A Management Information System (MIS): A formal method of making available to all levels of management appropriate, timely, accurate, and complete information to facilitate decision making and the planning, operational, and control functions of the organization.

Parts of an MIS: An MIS is complex, but its three major components are a Transaction Processing System (TPS), perhaps the most important part of an MIS; a Management Reporting System (MRS); and a Decision Support System (DSS).

Transaction Processing System (TPS): The transaction processing system organizes information about routine business transactions. A transaction is any activity or event that occurs in an organization or between the organization and its external environment—for example, ordering raw materials, paying rent or mortgage, or billing. A TPS is useful for a large number of repetitive transactions, with well-known, routine information and processing steps, often called **standard operating procedures (SOP)**. (A TPS is not involved in decision-making.)

Management Reporting System (MRS): Used for routine decisions. Most business decisions are routine in that both the decision-making factors and the information needed to make the decisions are well understood. This information can be put into a predetermined format and, through computer technology, processed to provide the routine reports needed for decision making. If information requirements change, the system must be adjusted.

Decision Support System (DSS): Used for decisions that are not routine and repetitive. Since the information necessary for such unstructured, nonroutine decisions is not the same or easy to recognize, the design of a DSS is difficult. The key is flexibility—a system that can process information in many different ways.

Key 68 Operating and using an MIS

OVERVIEW *Use of an MIS involves computer use that should be made as efficient and economical as possible, as through networking. As use of computer MIS has increased, certain managerial concerns regarding security, ready information access, health, and other problems have arisen.*

Computer use in an MIS: Each part of an MIS system uses computers—hardware and software.
- Computer **hardware** includes the equipment—the **input devices** that provide information to the central processing unit (e.g., punch card reader, keyboard); the **central processing unit (CPU)**—the heart of a computer, that acquires, sorts, manipulates and stores (in memory) data; and **output devices**—printer, monitor.
- **Software** is the **programs** of instruction that run the computer hardware. These programs control the acquisition, manipulation, storage, and retrieval of data.

Linking computers: Productivity can be increased and costs decreased by linking computers into a network that can share certain devices, such as printers and plotters. One widely used networking system is Local Area Network (LAN), which links computers and hardware to allow maximum efficiency.

Security of information: The increases in networking and in the number of people with access to computers—and data—has led to concerns about the security of information. Of most concern is intrusion into software—programming and data bases. Access to data may be limited by the use of **passwords** and **encryption of data** into **code** that must be unscrambled before it is usable.

Other problems associated with MIS-computer use: Other concerns centering on increasing computer use include the possible harmful effects on **health** of long-term exposure to cathode ray tubes and the need for computer programs to be **"user friendly"** and not too difficult to use. Since sophisticated satellite systems and advanced computer technology now allow transmission of data almost instantaneously—**real time data**—attention must also be given to continuous and uninterrupted flow of information and its effect on immediate decision-making.

Theme 17 MANAGING AN INTERNATIONAL BUSINESS

*A*s the world appears to shrink and our perspective becomes more global, more and more businesses have expanded beyond the borders of their own countries, becoming truly international.

Many multinational companies—companies established in one country doing business in another country—have arisen, and a whole new branch of management has evolved—that of international management. Knowledge of the reasons for international involvement, of the types of possible involvement, and of the problems unique to international business is essential for all managers in today's global world.

INDIVIDUAL KEYS IN THIS THEME

69 Reasons for entering international markets

---

70 Types of international businesses

---

71 Problems associated with international business

Key 69   Reasons for entering
international markets

OVERVIEW   *A company enters the international scene to gain an advantage—increase sales or lower costs—so that productivity and profitability are maximized.*

National advantages: A nation may have an **absolute advantage** because its environment (raw materials, labor supply, production capabilities) enables it to produce a specific product exclusively or most cheaply, or it may develop a **comparative advantage**, ability to produce a certain product or handle certain technologies better than other countries. An advantage must be maintained, and to do so, a company may enter foreign markets to gain access to raw materials, cheap labor, or more customers.

Proximity to raw materials: A company may enter a foreign country to secure economical and reliable access to natural resources needed as raw materials for its products. Locating a plant near the source of raw materials can eliminate transportation costs and other problems associated with long-distance shipment of materials.

Proximity to customers: A company producing a product sold exclusively or primarily in one country may want to produce the product in that country. Transportation costs are eliminated and marketing more closely linked to production.

Need to expand markets: Once a company has obtained its likely full market share in its own country, it may enter foreign markets to find new customers. Before entering a foreign market, managers must analyze the customs, buying habits, and wants of the potential customers.

Global marketing: Closely related to the need for expanded markets is the theory that, as the world appears to grow smaller and more interrelated, consumer interests and values concerning products are becoming more alike. This increasing similarity of preferences has led to a concept of global marketing in which companies create and market products for an international audience.

Labor savings: A company may enter the international scene to save labor costs. U.S. labor costs are among the highest in the world, and companies may save money by manufacturing products in other countries even when shipment costs are added.

Key 70 Types of international businesses

OVERVIEW *There are several ways in which a business may enter the international market. The company may simply export to a foreign country; it may have parts assembled in another country, or it may set up subsidiaries in a foreign country. Each system has its advantages and disadvantages for the parent company, but all involve the company with a foreign culture—and this has important managerial implications.*

An exporting company: The most common way in which a business enters the international market is exporting, which involves the shipment of goods to a foreign country.
- For most situations, a **general export license**, granted by the U.S. government, is needed.
- If the goods have possible military or strategic use or the nation to which goods are destined is unfriendly, a special **validated export license** is needed each time a shipment is planned.
- **Resident buying offices**, established by foreign countries in the United States, help with export details and currency exchanges.
- **Foreign freight forwarders**, who may combine several small shipments to a country into one economical large shipment, can also handle export details.

Assembly in a foreign country: In this type of international involvement, a company ships parts to a host country, where the final product is assembled. The savings for the parent company are primarily lower labor costs.

Foreign licensing: The parent company, or **licensor**, grants to a foreign country, the **licensee**, the right to use an exclusive technology, patent or process in exchange for money—either a percentage of profits or a fixed annual fee. The licensor makes little other investment but cannot be sure that quality standards will be maintained.

Foreign subsidiaries: To save labor costs and have easy access to markets and/or raw materials, a company may decide to open a factory in a foreign country. It may do this independently or as a **joint venture** with a local company in the host country, in which case involvement in local labor unions, social customs, and politics will likely ensue.

Key 71   Problems associated with international business

OVERVIEW   *Several problems are specific to the operation of an international business. An effective manager must be aware of these potential problems, act to avoid them if possible or handle them when they occur, and be flexible in dealings with foreign customs, workforce, and governments. Only then can the likelihood of success outweigh the risks.*

Language problems: Effective communication is essential to all business transactions. A difference in language is one of the most common and serious problems encountered in international business. Even with expert translators, idiomatic or slang terms can be misinterpreted, lead to serious problems.

Cultural differences: Even those fluent in the language of the country may be unfamiliar with certain customs and unintentionally offend their foreign business associates or do something that hampers negotiations. Knowledge of the social customs (e.g., as pertaining to food and drink and entertaining) and lack of cultural bias are absolute necessities for effective management in a foreign country.

Trade barriers: Many countries wish to protect their local industry from foreign business. Governments may do this in several ways:
* **embargo** forbids the entry of certain products into a country.
* A **tariff** places a tax on all goods imported. This raises the price of the imported product so that it is equal or higher than the locally made product.
* A **quota** limits the number of a specific foreign good allowed into a country.

Piracy: The theft of patents, trademarks, copyrights and other forms of intellectual property is a growing problem of international business. Blue jeans and other articles of clothing, drugs, videotapes, records, and other products are routinely copied. In many less developed nations, legal protection of intellectual property or punishment of offenders is minimal.

Differences in accounting procedures and control standards: Each country has its own generally accepted accounting principles, and often these procedures and the standards they use are not comparable between countries. These differences make it extremely difficult for managers to evaluate performance. Attempts to develop a common international language for accountants have not succeeded.

Availability of adequate skilled labor force: A company opening a plant or office in a foreign country may often need to train the local work force. The company may still have lower labor costs, and the training benefits the local country.

Theme 18 MANAGEMENT IN CHANGING TIMES

Since the 1950s, the nature of the work and the workplace has changed fundamentally. The size and makeup of the workforce have also changed dramatically. These changes challenge managers, who must adapt to them and learn new skills to be effective.

INDIVIDUAL KEYS IN THIS THEME

72 Demographics of contemporary workers

73 Changes in work and the workplace

Key 72 Demographics of contemporary workers

OVERVIEW *The characteristics of the worker has changed in the last few decades. A larger work force with more women, fewer teenagers, and more older people has necessitated changes in managerial policy and emphasis. Also, the need for a more highly educated and skilled workforce when a large percentage of the population is illiterate or unskilled is presenting new challenges to American management.*

Larger work force: The number of workers is increasing. This is due to the increase in the number of people who in the past did not join the work force; to immigration, both legal and illegal; and other factors.

Older work force: Because of a decline in the U.S. birthrate between 1960 and the late 1970s, the number of young people entering the workforce is declining. At the same time, there is a growing need for workers in businesses that have traditionally employed young people, like fast-food restaurants, so older people are being actively recruited—and are joining the work force.

More women in the work force: The traditional image of the working father and stay-at-home mother has given way to the two-paycheck family, in which both parents work. The number of households headed by women also has increased, and with that the number of women in the work force. The nature of the jobs held by women has also changed. More women are involved in technical, professional, and managerial positions.

Key 73   Changes in work and the workplace

OVERVIEW   *The nature of work, the basis of the U.S. economy, and the environment of work have all changed fundamentally during the last half of the twentieth century. These changes confront managers with challenges that they must meet if an organization is to succeed and have any competitive advantage over other organizations in this country or other countries.*

Shift from a manufacturing base to an information-based economy: Since about 1950, the U.S. economy has undergone a major structural change, changing from an economy based primarily on manufacturing to an economy based on information. The acquisition, storage, handling, and retrieval of information has become the main industry in the United States, with well over 65 percent of the workforce employed in information-related jobs.

Need for skilled work force: With the shift to an information-based economy has come the need for more highly skilled and better educated workers. The need for laborers and other unskilled workers has and will continue to decrease while the need for technical and professional workers as well as managers will increase. This fact has great impact on educational systems.

Change in the work environment: With the shift to an information-based economy has come a change in the workplace. The work environment is now likely to include sophisticated computer hardware and related equipment. A manager must now be **computer literate**.

Effect on management: Management has changed and must continue to change to meet the needs of a changed economy. Productivity must now be measured in different ways, ways not based on traditional manufacturing, or assembly-line, thinking. People skills—skills in communication, motivation, goal setting, and performance appraisal—are increasingly important.

GLOSSARY

absolute advantage　Concept that asserts that a country which can produce a product exclusively, or non-exclusively but more cheaply than others, possesses an absolute marketing advantage for that product.

accountability　The obligation to give account for the results expected.

Administrative Theory　The first application of scientific principles of management to the total organization (not to individual levels, tasks, or workers).

administrative decisions　Decisions usually made by mid-level managers, concerning tactical matters designed to accomplish top management's overall strategy.

authority　The power to act for someone else.

avoidance　A strategy management may practice to deal with organizational conflicts that includes nonattention or creating a total separation of the combatants or a partial separation that allows for only limited interaction.

Behavioral Approach　A school of management that emphasizes the improvement of worker efficiency through an understanding of the workers themselves as opposed to the work.

behavioral approach to leadership　Approach that asserts that leaders are made, not born, and that leadership can be learned.

behavioral controls　Those actions taken by management that seek to specify, evaluate, and correct human performance within the organization.

BEQ, or
**break-even
quantity**

The quantity of product sales needed to break even, or meet all the costs involved in producing the product.

BFOQ (bona fide occupational qualification)

Selection criteria used to hire a new employee, criteria that do not violate the laws against discrimination and that are job-related.

brainstorming

A problem-solving process in which group participants, when confronted with a problem, generate as many possible solutions without offering any criticism. (Criticism is deferred until all possible solutions have been put forth.)

break-even analysis

A managerial planning technique using fixed costs, variable costs, and the price of a product to determine the minimum units of sales necessary to break even, to pay the total costs involved. The necessary sales are called the BEQ, or break-even quantity.

budget

A formalized statement of the goals of an organization stated in financial terms. Budgets are useful managerial tools for evaluating organizational performance.

business ethics

Codes or standards that guide the actions of a company along legal and ethical lines and which seek to avoid actions deemed unethical and therefore unacceptable, even though perhaps legal, because these actions go against the accepted moral standards of the time and place.

career life planning

A process for planning career objectives, personal objectives, and long-term retirement objectives through an assessment of one's values, strengths, interests, and goals and relating these to various career/life options.

a career path

A progression of jobs within an organization, each of which develops business or technical skills necessary for the next position.

115

carrying costs   All costs incurred by the holding of an inventory of raw materials, including storage, insurance, theft allowance, spoilage allowance, and opportunity costs.

centralization   Characteristic of an organization in which a limited amount of authority is delegated.

change   The process of transforming the way an individual or organization acts from one set of behaviors to another. Change may be systematic or planned, or it may be implemented in a random manner.

Change Processes   The ways in which changes are accomplished. A change process may be imposed from above, or may be participative, depending on the organizational philosophy and the nature of the change.

Classical Approach   The earliest attempt to study management in a scientific manner. It emphasized worker efficiency achieved through the "one right way" to perform a task as determined by the expert who possesses a scientific understanding of the work achieved by methodic study.

coercive power   That organizational power based upon a manager's ability to punish an employee.

command groups   Groups formally created by an organization and featuring a designated leader and group members. Such groups adhere to the hierarchical authority principles of the formal group.

commanding   The way by which managers direct employee actions.

common vocabulary

Words that have formally defined meanings that are accepted by a specific group and which facilitate communication by eliminating or greatly limiting the connotative meanings of words.

comparative advantage

The principle that asserts that countries should specialize in producing those products in which they have the greatest advantage or the least disadvantage in relation to other countries.

compensation

A system for fairly and equitably rewarding each employee. Generally, compensation can be viewed as cash (i.e. salary) and non-cash (i.e. the value of all other benefits, such as sick leave, vacation, health and welfare benefits, tuition payments, and social security payments).

compromise

A management strategy for handling conflict that seeks a problem resolution that satisfies at least part of each party's position.

conflict

In the organizational setting, disagreement between two or more parties or between two or more positions as to how best achieve the organization's goals.

confrontation

A management strategy for handling conflict that features a thorough and frank discussion of the sources and types of conflict and the achievement of a resolution that is in the best interest of the group, but which may be at the expense of one or all of the conflicting parties.

Contingency Approach

School of management that asserts that the best management style depends on or is contingent on the leadership style of the leader in relationship to the needs of the specific situation.

contribution margin	The price of a product minus its variable costs $(P - VC)$.
controlling	The managerial function of evaluating employee effort and taking corrective action to better ensure the accomplishment of the organization's goals.
control process	Sequential actions taken by management to establish performance standards, measure and evaluate performance, and take corrective action where indicated.
coordinating	The managerial function which creates a relationship between all the organization's efforts (individual tasks) in order to accomplish the common organizational goal.
corporate culture	The sum total of the values, customs, traditions, and meanings that make a company unique; often called the "character of an organization".
CPU, or **Central Processing Unit**	The basic electronic unit of a computer which performs the desired calculations to acquire, sort, calculate, manipulate and store data.
critical incident logs	Diaries of employee actions that are considered critical examples of either good or bad performance, used by managers to evaluate employee performance.
critical path	The longest path through a PERT network that is the shortest time for total project completion.
decentralization	Characteristic of an organization in which a significant amount of authority is delegated to lower levels in the organization.

decision-making process The sequence of events taken by management to solve managerial problems, a systematic process that follows a sequence of: problem identification, alternative solutions generation, consequences analysis, solution selection and implementation, evaluation and feedback.

delegation The art of assigning responsibilities to others together with the delegated authority commensurate with the responsibilities for the accomplishment of results.

demographics The science of measuring and analyzing data about the population. It relies heavily upon survey research and census data.

demography The study of populations.

departmentalization The grouping of related functions into manageable units to achieve the objectives of the enterprise in the most efficient and effective manner.

development The human resource function which emphasizes preparing employees to develop skills to better perform their current job and to enhance their abilities to perform additional or more difficult jobs in the organization.

discretionary time Time regulated by one's own choice, time in which one is free to do what one wishes.

division of labor The division of work and functions into smaller activities.

dominance (Power intervention) a management strategy for handling conflicts in which a solution is imposed by management higher than the level at which the conflict exists.

Economic Order Quantity (EOQ) Model Model that relates carrying costs of inventory, ordering, and usage to determine the most economical size of inventory.

efficiency   The amount of worker output in a given period of time. It is a measure of how well organizational resources are used. The greater the output, the more efficient the worker is.

essay appraisals   A form of employee performance evaluation that requires the evaluator to write a formal essay citing what the employee has done and providing an evaluation.

Expectancy Theory   A theory of motivation, developed by Victor Vroom, that attempts to explain behavior in terms of an individual's goals and his/her expectations of achieving those goals.

expert power   The degree of influence held by an individual in an organization because the expertise possessed by the individual is needed and therefore valued by the organization.

external environment   Those factors outside an organization that influence it and interact with each other. The factors are primarily economic, political, sociological and state-of-the-art technology.

feedback   Information about job performance derived from the job itself that is used in a corrective manner.

filtering   The altering of a message as it passes through the personalities of either the sender or the receiver.

financial controls   Formally states financial objectives of an organization setting forth, for a defined period of time, the financial parameters within which it will operate, the conditions assumed to exist during that time, and performance standards against which financial performance is to be judged.

fixed costs   Those costs which do not vary with the level of production.

formal group

A group that has the sanction of the organization within which it exists, possesses legitimate power within the organization, and generally is formed to accomplish a designated task or function.

formal leader

One who is officially assigned leadership responsibilities within the organization.

functional definition of management

Definition of management in terms of its functions: planning, organizing, commanding, coordinating, and controlling.

GAAP (Generally Accepted Accounting Principles)

Standards of accounting practice developed in an individual country that furnish a standard by which accounting statements may be evaluated. They vary greatly from country to country.

GATT (General Agreement on Tariffs and Trade)

An international treaty among the leading industrial nations that is administered through a permanent organization called a secretariat. It is through this permanent organization that member nations act to reduce tariff and trading barriers.

general export license

License that confers upon an exporter the right to send goods overseas; it is generally good for an entire category of goods.

genetic approach to leadership

Approach based on the idea that leaders are born, not made.

global marketing

A concept, popularized by Theodore Levitt, that stresses that what people value in product characteristics are converging or becoming alike. This convergence of preference becomes the basis for universal marketing of products with the same or similar marketing techniques no matter what the country.

goal

A long range aim.

Gross National Product (GNP)	The most widely accepted measure of a nation's productivity; it consists of the value of all goods and services produced in a country in a year.
group norms	Forms of behavior, ideals, or opinions that are expected within the group as being acceptable and desirable.
hardware	All physical devices of a computer system (e.g., CPU, monitor, printer, disk drive etc.) that input data, store data, and output data.
Hawthorne Studies	Famous human relations experiments conducted between 1927 and 1932 by Elton Mayo and his colleagues at the Hawthorne (Chicago) Works of the Western Electric Company, that demonstrated the importance of human relations for increased productivity.
hierarchy of objective	A managerial concept that views the different levels or magnitudes of decision-making within an organization structure in terms of a hierarchy of objectives to be achieved.
human relation factors	The social and psychological factors that influence organizational functioning.
Human Resource Management	The term generally applied to those activities concerning the management of people.
IFCA (Information For Competitive Advantage)	A dynamic view of information that stresses that information is valuable to management because it confers competitive advantages in the marketplace.
incremental innovation	A process of introducing change into an organization in which, to minimize resistance, the proposed change is broken down into small steps or "increments".

informal group Two or more people affiliated in a group that is not officially sanctioned by the organization.

innovative objectives Objectives that involve solving a special problem, starting a new project, or dealing with non-recurring assignments.

input controls Corrective actions taken during the input phase of the organization's activities; also referred to as **steering controls**.

internal environment Those factors inside an organization, an organization's resources, primarily financial, physical, human, and current technology factors.

interest group An informal workplace group consisting of individuals who affiliate because of a common interest.

JIT (just in time) An approach to inventory management derived from Japan in which needed raw materials inventory arrives exactly when it is to be used, or ''just in time.''

job design The science of arranging the components of a total task in the most efficient manner.

job enrichment A job design technique that seeks to improve worker motivation and ultimately job performance by implementing more creative, challenging, responsible, autonomous jobs that give workers greater recognition and satisfaction.

job fractionation A term coined by Frederick W. Taylor to describe the process of breaking a job into its component parts.

job interview

A face-to-face meeting between two persons for the purpose of exploring mutual interests pertaining to a job. It is a structured conversation which allows the interviewer to assess the applicant's potential and the applicant to assess whether or not the job is for him or her.

job satisfaction

An individual's general attitude and feeling about his/her job.

job specialization, or division of labor

The belief that productivity results from employees' specializing in specific jobs and developing the skills necessary to perform those jobs.

LAN (Local Area Network)

A methodology employing both hardware and software to link computers to enable sharing of individual components and maximal efficiency of equipment use.

linear thinking

An approach to problem solving that assumes that each problem has a single solution, that the solution will only affect the problem and not the rest of the organization, and that once implemented, a solution will remain valid and should be evaluated only on how well it solves the problem.

link-pin view of an organization

A conceptualization of **Rensis Likert** in which a large organization is seen as a series of interrelated groups.

long-range objectives

Objectives that extend beyond the current budget cycle of the organization.

long range planning

Planning that analyzes alternatives to achieving the mission. In long range planning outputs are usually targets of opportunity within the industry or market.

management

Working with and through other people to accomplish the objectives of both the organization and its members.

management activities	The functions of planning, organizing, staffing, coordinating, motivating, leading, and controlling in order to get results effectively through other people by the process of delegation.
Management by Objectives (MBO)	A systematic approach that allows management to focus on achievable goals and to attain the best possible results from available resources.
Management Science	A school of management thought that emerged in the 1940s and stressed a scientific approach to productivity improvement resulting in many widely used techniques for the management of production and operations **(POM)**.
managerial audit	A formal evaluation of the effectiveness of managerial practices within an organization.
Managerial Grid	A practical methodology developed by Drs. Blake and Mouton making use of the University of Michigan dimensions of leadership, to categorize the leadership styles of managers.
managerial strategy	Strategy concerned with the long-term goals and objectives of the enterprise and the allocation of resources and the adoption of appropriate courses of action to carry out these goals.
maximin solution to the payoff table	A pessimistic view that asserts that the desirable course of action is that which leads to the best (maximum) of worst (minimum) results.
maximax solution to a payoff table	The most optimistic view, which assumes that the desired result will be the best possibility of all the favorable results.

MIS (Management Information System)	A system that integrates all people, procedures, data and equipment of an organization into a comprehensive system that produces all the required information for all levels within the organization.
multi-national company (MNC)	A company established in one country (parent country) and doing business in a foreign country (host country).
model	A mathematical simulation of a real-world situation/environment that is a useful planning tool.
motivation	The process of stimulating an individual to take action that will accomplish a desired goal.
Motivation-Maintenance Theory	A theory of motivation formulated by Frederick Herzberg, that states that all work-related factors can be grouped into one of two categories: maintenance (hygiene) factors, which will not produce motivation and can prevent it, and motivator factors, which motivate workers.
MRP (Materials Requirements Planning)	A technique for determining the amount, quality, and timing of the components used in the manufacturing process; often used with **CRP** (Capacity Requirements Planning) which takes the materials required and converts them into "standard work hours" on the labor and equipment of work centers to effectively schedule the work required.
need hierarchy	The five different levels of individual needs identified by Abraham H. Maslow in his theory of motivation; namely, physiological, safety, social, esteem or ego, and self-actualization.
noise	Anything that changes a message but is not part of either the sender or receiver.

126

non-programmed decisions
Decisions concerning problems that are not well understood nor highly structured but tend to be unique and do not lend themselves to routine or systematic procedures.

objective
A result expected by the end of the budget cycle.

one right way
Phrase coined by Frederick W. Taylor to describe the method of performing a work task determined by the scientific manager. This one correct way of performing a job was derived from time and motion studies and other measures. A job for which the one right way had been determined was said to have been "Taylorized."

Open Systems Model
A view of an organization dynamically and continually interacting with its environment as it takes inputs, acts to transform those inputs, and produces outputs.

operational decisions
Decisions made by supervisors who determine the day-to-day operations of an organization.

operational planning
Or day-to-day planning, planning that addresses specific timetables and measurable targets.

ordering costs
All costs associated with the ordering of inventory, including clerical labor, forms, and processing costs.

organization
The tool that makes it possible for a group or team to work together more effectively than they might work alone in order to achieve goals.

Organizational Climate
The overall environment of an organizational entity; it takes into account power structure, external forces, and perceived needs.

Organizational Development	The concept of changing the behavior of an organization, either in its entirety or in parts, by changing the way employees work, by changing the structure of the organization, or by changing the technology used.
organizational power	Those kinds of power sanctioned within the organizational structure and used by managers. Organizational power includes legitimate power, reward power, coercive power, expert power, referent power, and information power.
organizational purpose	The reason the business is in existence, the primary objective of the organization.
organizing	The way in which the organization is structured. Traditionally organization is along functional, geographic, product or customer (end-user) lines or a hybrid of these forms.
output controls	The actions taken by management to regulate an organization's output of either goods or services or both.
payoff matrix, or **decision table**	A formal arrangement showing the relationship between managerial choices, external conditions (states of demand), the probability of occurrence of these external conditions, and the probable payoff, or profit, from the various courses of managerial action; a planning tool to aid management in choosing a specific strategy or course of action by evaluating potential returns.
peer group	Also known as a **friendship group,** an informal group of employees who meet outside the workplace and are united by a common interest, such as a hobby.
performance contract	Agreement made between a manager and his/her subordinate concerning the

responsibilities of the subordinate and the standards by which the subordinate is to be judged for that budget cycle.

PERT (Project Evaluation Review Technique)
A network model that aids management in determining the correct and most economically efficient sequence of tasks for completion of a project.

planning
The management function consisting of forecasting future events and determining the most effective activities for the total organization to achieve its objectives.

policies
General broad guidelines for action to attain specific goals.

Principles of Management
14 guidelines for managers, developed by Henri Fayol. They include division of labor (work specialization), authority, discipline, unity of command, unity of direction, subordination of the individual, remuneration, centralization, scalar chain, order, equity, stability of personnel, initiative, and esprit de corps.

price follower
A company that prices its goods or services in the marketplace by imitating or "following" the existing market leaders.

price leader
A company that sets the price for a good or service offered in the marketplace.

proactive adaptation
An approach to social responsibility in which a company anticipates future social problems and acts to deal with these future problems before they become significant.

problem avoider (smoother)
Manager who seeks to preserve the status quo and to avoid having to deal with problems within the organization, by ignoring or smoothing over problems.

problem seeker
Manager who actively anticipates problems and acts to deal with them before they develop.

problem solver
The normative managerial type who, when confronted with a problem, seeks its solution.

process controls
Those control actions which impact upon the organization's internal processes and serve to regulate and evaluate transformational activities.

production bonus
Payment above and beyond the normal piece rate offered to workers to motivate extra productivity.

programmed decisions
Decisions involving problems that are well understood, highly structured, routine, and repetitive and that lend themselves to systematic procedures and rules.

QC (Quality Circles)
Small groups of workers and management that meet on a regular basis during the regular workday and attempt to improve quality and help cut costs by making creative suggestions to top management.

reactive adaptation
An approach to social responsibility in which a company ''reacts'' to current social problems.

recruitment
The human resources acquisition process by which an organization attracts and hires suitable employees.

Recruitment and Selection
The process by which a new employee or new employees are attracted to the organization and are chosen to fill specific positions.

referent power
The form or power within an organization exercised by an individual by virtue of personal character; often called *charisma*.

research and audit	Activites undertaken to assess efficiency and effectiveness. Research and Audit studies form a factual basis for decisions about future programs as well as ensuring compliance with current regulations.
resistance to change	A force, active in individuals and in groups, that tends to minimize or limit the amount of change which will occur.
responsibility	The duty or task to be performed.
resume	An individual written summary of personal, educational, and experience qualifications intended to demonstrate an applicant's fitness for a particular position or positions; a digest of qualifications for a job.
reward power	Power within an organization held by an individual who has the ability to confer rewards.
routine objectives	Objectives that are on-going, that occur from year-to-year.
scalar principle	Idea that there should be a clear definition of authority in an organization and that this authority flows, one link at a time, through a chain of command from top to bottom in the organization.
separation	The functional term describing the manner in which an employee leaves an organization.
sequential events	Those steps of a task which must be performed in a specified order.
simultaneous events	Those steps of a task which can be performed at the same time.

smokestack America	A popular term used to describe the traditional manufacturing core of U.S. industry; examples of "smokestack" industries are the steel, coal, automotive industries.
smoothing	A management technique for handling conflict that stresses the achievement of harmony between the disputants. Treating a problem superficially, denying its importance to the organization, or complete denial that a problem exists are examples of smoothing.
social audit	The dynamic process by which an organization evaluates its level of social responsibility activities.
Social Obligation Approach	Approach to social responsiveness that assumes that the main goals of a business are economic success and not the meeting of social obligations and therefore that business should merely meet the minimal social obligations imposed by current legislation.
Social Responsibility Approach	Approach to social responsiveness that assumes that the goals of business are not merely economic but also social and that business should devote economic resources to the accomplishment of social goals.
social responsiveness	The extent to which an organization is responsive to its perceived social obligations, generally a measure of business effectiveness and efficiency in pursuing actions which meet social obligations.
Social Responsiveness Approach	Approach to social responsiveness that assumes that business not only has economic and social goals but must also anticipate future social problems and act now to respond to those future problems.

software

Programs of instructions that control the actions of the hardware components of a computer system. Functions such as data acquisition, processing and manipulation and storage are facilitated and controlled by software programs.

span of control

The number of employees a manager can supervise effectively; the number of subordinates supervised by one manager, generally expressed as a ratio of manager-to-employees (e.g., a span of control of 1:4 means that a manager is supervising 4 employees); also known as **span of management**.

standard of performance

A statement of what will occur when a responsibility is carried out well.

strategic decisions

Decisions, usually made by top management, that determine the nature of an organization's business; also referred to as "business policy decisions."

strategic planning

planning that addresses the mission of the organization in terms of its main business. Outputs of strategic planning include broad, general guidelines—for example, which markets to pursue.

structural change

A fundamental shift from one kind of productive activity to another. Selling a steel factory and using the money to create a data processing company represents a structural change, a change from manufacturing to information processing. However, selling a steel factory and using the money to open a factory to manufacture teflon-coated pots is not a structural change; it is merely a shifting from one kind of manufacturing activity to another.

subordinate-imposed time	Time that a manager spends performing tasks that rightfully belong to his/her subordinates; a form of reverse delegation.
systems thinking	A contemporary and complex approach to problem solving that assumes that problems are complex and related to a situation; that solutions not only solve the problem but will also impact on the rest of the organization; that solutions should be evaluated on how well they solve the problem (intended results) and how they affect the total organization (unintended results); and that neither problems nor solutions remain constant: situations change, problems change, and new solutions are always needed.
task groups	Groups formally created by an organization to accomplish a specific project.
technical activities	Activities or tasks that are the special function of an individual or the following of his/her vocational field.
therbligs	A term coined by **Frank Gilbreth**, an early pioneer in the use of **time and motion studies**, to describe the seventeen categories of worker motion used in job accomplishment.
theories of leadership	Various ways in which the source of leadership has been understood and include a genetic derivation of leadership, a trait theory of leadership, a behavioral explanation of leadership, and situational theories of leadership.
Theory X	A characterization of the traditional view of the worker as lazy, not motivated, disliking work, seeking security, not really creative, and possessing limited intellectual capacities.
Theory Y	A characterization of Douglas M. McGregor of a more contemporary and humanistic view

of the worker as responsible, committed to accepting challenging, truly creative, trustworthy, seeking new challenge, and capable of learning to accept responsibility.

Theory Z, or **Japanese Management Theory**
Theory that stresses decision-making by group consensus and places emphasis on achievement of the group rather than the individual worker.

trait theory of leadership
A genetic based theory that asserts that leadership is derived from inherited traits.

transformation process
What occurs within an organization as it takes inputs (raw materials) and changes them into an output (goods or services). The transformational process is a valued-added process so that the output is worth more in the marketplace than the input factors.

unity of command
Term for the idea that an employee should have one and only one immediate boss.

utility
An economic concept that refers to value derived by the customer or end-user. **Time utility** is the value placed by a customer on being able to purchase a product at the appropriate time. **Form utility** is the value placed by consumers on having a product in the correct form. **Place utility** is the value placed by the customer on having a product in the correct place or location.

validated export license
A formal government permission for the export of a specific commodity that is deemed of strategic value (valuable and rare) or of potential military application or for the export of products of any nature to a country deemed unfriendly to the United States.

variable costs
Those costs of production that vary directly with the number of units produced, generally direct labor and direct material costs.

INDEX